GALATIANS
FOR YOU

TIMOTHY KELLER
GALATIANS
FOR YOU

thegoodbook
COMPANY

Galatians For You

© Timothy Keller, 2013

Published by:
The Good Book Company

Tel (US): 866 244 2165
Tel (UK): 0333 123 0880
International: +44 (0) 208 942 0880
Email: admin@thegoodbook.co.uk

Websites:

North America: www.thegoodbook.com
UK: www.thegoodbook.co.uk
Australia: www.thegoodbook.com.au
New Zealand: www.thegoodbook.co.nz

ISBN:9781908762573

Design by André Parker

Printed in the USA

CONTENTS

SERIES PREFACE

Each volume of the *God's Word For You* series takes you to the heart of a book of the Bible, and applies its truths to your heart.

The central aim of each title is to be:

- Bible centered
- Christ glorifying
- Relevantly applied
- Easily readable

You can use *Galatians For You:*

To read. You can simply read from cover to cover, as a book that explains and explores the themes, encouragements and challenges of this part of Scripture.

To feed. You can work through this book as part of your own personal regular devotions, or use it alongside a sermon or Bible-study series at your church. Each chapter is divided into two shorter sections, with questions for reflection at the end of each.

To lead. You can use this as a resource to help you teach God's word to others, both in small-group and whole-church settings. You'll find tricky verses or concepts explained using ordinary language, and helpful themes and illustrations along with suggested applications.

These books are not commentaries. They assume no understanding of the original Bible languages, nor a high level of biblical knowledge. Verse references are marked in **bold** so that you can refer to them easily. Any words that are used rarely or differently in everyday language outside the church are marked in gray when they first appear, and are explained in a glossary toward the back. There, you'll also find details of resources you can use alongside this one, in both personal and church life.

Our prayer is that as you read, you'll be struck not by the contents of this book, but by the book it's helping you open up; and that you'll praise not the author of this book, but the One he is pointing you to.

Carl Laferton, Series Editor

INTRODUCTION TO GALATIANS

The book of Galatians is dynamite. It is an explosion of joy and freedom which leaves us enjoying a deep significance, security and satisfaction—the life of blessing God calls His people into.

Why? Because it brings us face to face with the gospel. It's very common in Christian circles to assume that "the gospel" is something mainly for non-Christians. We see it as a set of basic "ABC" doctrines that are the way in which someone enters the kingdom of God. We often assume that once we're converted, we don't need to hear or study or understand the gospel—we need more "advanced" material.

But in this short letter, Paul outlines the bombshell truth that *the gospel is the A to Z of the Christian life*. It is not only the way to *enter* the kingdom; it is the way to *live* as part of the kingdom. It is the way Christ transforms people, churches and communities.

> The gospel is not only the way to enter the kingdom; it is the way to live in the kingdom.

We're going to see Paul showing the young Christians in Galatia that their spiritual problem is not only caused by *failing to* live in obedience to God, but also by *relying on* obedience to Him. We're going to see him telling them that all they need—all they could ever need—is the gospel of God's unmerited favor to them through Christ's life, death and resurrection. We're going to hear him solving their issues not through telling them to "be better Christians", but by calling them to live out the implications of the gospel.

We're going to watch Paul challenge them, and us, with the simple truth that the gospel is not just the ABC of Christianity, but the A to Z—that Christians need the gospel just as much as non-Christians.

Paul will explain to us that the truths of the gospel change life from top to bottom; that they transform our hearts, our thinking and our approach to absolutely everything. The gospel—the message that we are more wicked than we ever dared believe, but more loved and accepted in Christ than we ever dared hope—creates a radical new dynamic for personal growth, for obedience, for love.

Galatians is all about the gospel, which all of us need throughout all of our lives. It's dynamite, and I pray that it explodes in your heart, and makes you passionate to see it do the same work in others' hearts, as you read this book.

Below, I've briefly summarized the historical setting of the letter; and in an appendix, I've touched on some modern debates over its message. But if at this point you want to get into Galatians itself, turn to page 13.

Timothy Keller

The historical context

The apostle Paul was a church-planting missionary. After he planted a church and left a region, he continued to supervise new congregations through his letters. One of these letters is this epistle to the Christian churches in the area of Galatia in Asia Minor. Most scholars agree that this letter was written by Paul around AD50 (only 15-20 years after the death of Christ). It is helpful to recognize the following three things from the historical setting, which will help us understand this epistle:

■ This letter addresses a social and racial division in the churches of Galatia. The first Christians in Jerusalem were Jewish, but as the gospel spread out from that center, increasing numbers of Gentiles began to receive Christ. However, a group of teachers in Galatia were now insisting that the Gentile Christians practice all the traditional ceremonial customs of the law of Moses, as the Jewish Christians did. They taught that the Gentiles had to observe all the dietary laws and be circumcised for full acceptance and to be completely pleasing to God.

■ Although this specific controversy may seem remote to us today, Paul addressed it with an abiding, all-important truth. He taught that the cultural divisions and disunity in the Galatian churches were due to a confusion about the nature of the gospel. By insisting on Christ-plus-anything-else as a requirement for full acceptance by God, these teachers were presenting a whole different way of relating to God (a "different gospel", 1:6) from the one Paul had given them ("the one we preached", 1:8). It is this different gospel that was creating the cultural division and strife. Paul forcefully and unapologetically fought the "different gospel" because to lose one's grip of the true gospel is to desert and lose Christ Himself (1:6). Therefore, everything was at stake in this debate.

■ The most obvious fact about the historical setting is often the most overlooked. In the letter to the Galatians, Paul expounds in detail what the gospel is and how it works. But the intended audience of this exposition of the gospel are all professing Christians. It is not simply non-Christians but also believers who need continually to learn the gospel and apply it to their lives.

1. THE UNIQUENESS OF THE GOSPEL

Perhaps the most striking aspect of the opening of Galatians is Paul's tone, and the frame of mind that lies behind it. He is surprised. And he also seems angry. His language, almost from the outset, is remarkably strong. Where normally Paul's letters move on, after his greeting, to a thanksgiving for those he's writing to (see, for example, Philippians 1:3-8; Colossians 1:3-8; 1 Corinthians 1:4-9), here he simply says: "I am astonished…" (**verse 6a***). What has made Paul so emotional?

Desertion

First, Paul is astonished because these young Christians are taking hold of a **gospel†** that isn't really a gospel (**v 7**), so they are in enormous danger. They are in "confusion" (**v 7b**).

Second, he is directly angry at the ones who are misleading the converts of the church—those who are "trying to pervert the gospel" (**v 7b**). He calls down condemnation on them (**v 9**). More indirectly, he is also angry at the Galatian Christians themselves, warning them that they are deserting the God who called them (**v 6b**)—a serious charge!

We'll see as we walk through Paul's letter that what caused his opening outburst was a group of teachers who were teaching Gentile Christian converts that they were obliged to keep the Jewish cultural customs of the **Mosaic law**—the dietary laws, circumcision and the rest of the

---

* All Galatians verse references being looked at in each chapter are in **bold**.
† Words in **gray** are defined in the Glossary (page 187).

ceremonial law in order to be truly pleasing to God. To the Galatians, this probably didn't appear to be a radical difference from what they'd been taught. Surely the whole point of the Christian life is to be pleasing to God! But Paul says: *This is an absolute repudiation of all that I have been telling you.*

He is not pulling his punches! But if we believe what Paul believed about the gospel, then we will find his attitude justifiable. If the Galatians are really turning their backs on God and taking hold of a gospel that isn't a gospel at all, then their condition is dangerous. The anxiety and anger that Paul expresses is the same that any loving parent or friend would experience if a child or companion was going seriously astray.

Paul's Right to Speak

But *who* is Paul to write to these Christians in this way?

An "apostle" (**v 1**)—a man who has been sent with *immediate divine authority.* The Greek word *apostolos* means to be "sent". Paul's phrase "not from men nor by man" drives home the uniqueness of the first apostles. Those who are called to ministry by the Holy Spirit today are not "from men" either—the ultimate cause of their ministry is Jesus' call, and the ultimate authority for their ministry is Jesus' word in the Bible. But they are appointed "by man". (The Greek word here—*dia*—means "by" or "through", as in our word "diameter".) This means that though ministers ultimately receive their call from God, they are called *through* the intermediaries of other human ministers, or *through* the election of a congregation, and so on.

Paul is claiming something more than this for himself. He is saying that he did not receive his apostolic **commission** through anyone else at all. No other apostles commissioned him. He was commissioned and taught *directly by the risen Jesus Himself* (see Acts 9:1-19).

Second, in **verses 8-9**, Paul says he was sent with a *particular divine message*—the gospel. This means his divine teaching is the standard for judging who is **orthodox** and who is **heretical**, as he says in **verse 9**: "If anybody is preaching to you a gospel other than what you accepted, let him be eternally condemned!" Even an apostle cannot alter, revise or add to the message of Christ. What he says is not the result of his study, research, reflection and wisdom. It is God-given, and both unchanging and unchangeable.

We might wonder: are there any more apostles today? Not in the full way of Paul and **the Twelve**. In the early church, others were called "apostles of the churches" (for example, 2 Corinthians 9:3). Barnabas was "sent" to Antioch, and in that sense was an "apostle" (Acts 11:22, and see also Acts 14:14). However, while they were sent out as missionaries, they were commissioned by the other, original apostles or by the churches—"by man". Barnabas never met the risen Christ; he was never taught and tutored in the gospel by the bodily-present Christ, as Paul and the Twelve were. So we can call people who have unusual leadership gifts, then and now, "small-a" apostles. But Paul is a "capital-A" Apostle, commissioned directly by Jesus. The "capital-A" Apostles had, and have, absolute authority. What *they* write is Scripture.

What is the Gospel?

And so this divinely appointed Apostle reminds the Galatian Christians of his particular divine message—the gospel. In his opening, he gives them a quick, yet pretty comprehensive, outline of the gospel message:

Who we are: Helpless and lost. That is what the word "rescue" implies in **verse 4**. Other founders of religions came to teach, not to rescue. Jesus was a great teacher, but when Paul gives us this nutshell version of Jesus' ministry, he makes *no* mention of that at all. The average person on the street believes that a Christian is someone who follows Christ's teaching and example. But Paul implies that's impossible. After all, you don't rescue people unless they are in a lost state and a helpless condition! Imagine you see a drowning woman. It doesn't help her at all if you throw her a manual on how to swim. You don't throw her some teaching—you throw her a rope. And Jesus is not so much a teacher as He is a rescuer. Because that's what we most need. Nothing in who we are or what we do saves us. This is what theologians call "spiritual inability".

What Jesus did: How did Jesus rescue us? He "gave himself for our **sins**" (**v 4a**). He made a sacrifice which was **substitutionary** in nature. The word "for" means "on behalf of" or "in place of". Substitution is why the gospel is so revolutionary. Christ's death was not just a general sacrifice, but a substitutionary one. He did not merely buy us a "second chance", giving us another opportunity to get life right and stay right with God. He did *all* we needed to do, but cannot do. If Jesus' death really paid for our sins on our behalf, we can never fall back into condemnation. Why? Because God would then be getting two payments for the same sin, which is unjust! Jesus did all we should have done, in our place, so when He becomes our Savior, we are absolutely free from penalty or condemnation.

> Substitution is why the gospel is so revolutionary.

What the Father did: God accepted the work of Christ on our behalf by raising Him "from the dead" (**v 1**) and by giving us the "**grace** and peace" (**v 3**) that Christ won and achieved for us.

Why God did it: This was all done out of grace—not because of anything we have done, but "according to the will of our God and Father" (**v 4d**). We did not ask for rescue, but God in His grace planned what we didn't realize we needed, and Christ by His grace (**v 6**) came to achieve the rescue we could never have achieved ourselves.

There is no indication of any other motivation or cause for Christ's mission except the will of God. There is nothing in us which merits it. Salvation is sheer *grace.*

That is why the only one who gets "glory for ever" is God alone (**v 5**). If we contributed to our rescue... if we had rescued ourselves...

or if God had seen something deserving of rescue, or useful for His plan, in us… or even if we had simply called out for rescue based on our own reasoning and understanding… then we could pat ourselves on the back for the part we played in saving ourselves.

But the biblical gospel—Paul's gospel—is clear that salvation, from first to last, is God's doing. It is His calling; His plan; His action; His work. And so it is He who deserves all the glory, for all time.

This is the humbling truth that lies at the heart of Christianity. We love to be our own saviors. Our hearts love to manufacture glory for themselves. So we find messages of self-salvation extremely attractive, whether they are religious (*Keep these rules and you earn eternal blessing*) or secular (*Grab hold of these things and you'll experience blessing now*). The gospel comes and turns them all upside down. It says: *You are in such a hopeless position that you need a rescue that has nothing to do with you at all.* And then it says: *God in Jesus provides a rescue which gives you far more than any false salvation your heart may love to chase.*

Paul reminds us that in the gospel we are both brought lower and raised higher than we can imagine. And the glory for that, rightly, all goes to "our God and Father … for ever and ever. **Amen**" (**v 5**).

Questions for reflection

1. Paul's tone reminds us that Christian faith is a matter of heart, as well as head—feelings, as well as intellect. How does this encourage you? How does it challenge you?

2. When do you find it hardest to accept the authority of apostolic New Testament teaching? Why?

3. How would you explain the gospel to someone who asked you today what you believe?

PART TWO

Gospel Revision = Gospel Reversal

The biblical gospel of grace is a precious thing. And it's this glorious gospel that the Galatian churches' leaders have been perverting, and that the Galatian church members have been deserting.

This matters because Paul says that any such change to *the* gospel means it becomes "*no* gospel at all" (**verse 7**). Why is this? Why is it that any change to the gospel, however small, makes it null and void?

Because, Paul says, Christians were "called … by the grace of Christ" (**v 6**). God called us; we didn't call Him. And God accepted us right away despite our lack of merit. That is the order of the gospel. God accepts us, and *then* we follow Him. But other religious systems have it the other way around. We must give God something, and *then* He accepts us. So in **verse 7**, Paul says that any teaching which adds keeping Mosaic ceremonial law to faith in Christ "perverts" the gospel. Literally, the word he chooses to use means "reverses".

This is illuminating. If you add *anything* to Christ as a requirement for acceptance with God—if you start to say: *To be saved I need the grace of Christ* **plus** *something else*—you completely reverse the "order" of the gospel and make it null and void. Any revision of the gospel reverses it. That is why in **verse 6** Paul says that the false teachers are producing "a different gospel", which he quickly qualifies in **verse 7** as "really no gospel at all". Literally, Paul says: "*another gospel, which is not another*".

This is crystal clear. Another gospel is not another gospel. It is *no* gospel. To change the gospel the tiniest bit is to lose it so completely that the new teaching has no right to be called a "gospel". The sixteenth-century Reformer Martin Luther summed it up well:

"There is no middle ground between Christian **righteousness** and **works-righteousness.** There is no other alternative to Christian righteousness but works righteousness; if you do not

build your confidence on the work of Christ you must build
your confidence on your own work."

(*Commentary on the Epistle to the Galatians*, Preface)

Losing the Gospel Today

What Paul battled in his day, and Luther fought against in his, we witness in ours, too. Remember, Paul condemns any teaching that is not
based on the fact that:

- we are too sinful to contribute to our salvation (we need a
  complete rescue).
- we are saved by belief in Jesus' work—the "grace of Christ"—
  plus nothing else.

Here are three examples of current views that deny one or both of
these two truths:

1. In some churches, it is implicitly or explicitly taught that *you are
   saved through your "surrender" to Christ, plus right beliefs and behavior.* This is a fairly typical mistake in evangelical churches. People
   are challenged to "give your life to Jesus" and/or to "ask Him into
   your life." This sounds very biblical, but it still can reject the grace-
   first principle fairly easily. People think that we are saved by a strong
   belief and trust in and love for God, along with a life committed
   to Him. Therefore, they feel they must begin by generating a high
   degree of spiritual sorrow, hunger, and love in order to get Christ's
   presence. Then they must somehow maintain this if they are going
   to "stay saved". So functionally—that is, in actual reality—a church
   is teaching the idea that we are saved because of the level of our
   faith. But the gospel says that we are saved *through* our faith. The
   first approach really makes our performance the savior, and the
   second makes Christ's performance the Savior. It is not the level but
   the *object* of our faith that saves us.

2. In other churches, it is taught that *it doesn't really matter what you
   believe as long as you are a loving and good person.* This is a typical mistake in "liberal" churches. This view teaches that all good

people, regardless of their religion (or lack of one), will find God. This sounds extremely open-minded on the surface, but it is actually intolerant of grace, in two ways.

First, it teaches that good works are enough to get to God. If all good people can know God, then Jesus' death was not necessary; all it takes is virtue. The trouble is, this means bad people have no hope, contradicting the gospel, which invites "both good and bad" to God's feast (Matthew 22:10). If you say people are saved by being good, then only "the good" can come in to God's feast. The gospel offer becomes exclusive, not inclusive.

> If good people can know God, Jesus' death was not necessary.

Second, it encourages people to think that if they are tolerant and open, they are pleasing to God. They don't *need* grace—they get eternal life for themselves. And so "glory for ever" (**v 5**) goes to them, for being good enough for heaven. The gospel, however, challenges people to see their radical sin. Without that sense of one's own evil, the knowledge of God's grace will not be transforming, and we will not understand how much God is glorified by the presence of *anyone at all* in heaven.

3. A third example is found in churches that are *extremely intolerant of small differences of dress or custom*. The false teachers of Galatia wanted (as we will see) to impose many old rules and regulations having to do with dress, diet and ritual observances. It is natural for us to associate them with highly regulated churches and religious communities which control their members very tightly and direct them into the "right" way to eat, dress, date, schedule their time, and so on. Or they may insist on a detailed observance of many complicated rituals. Modern-day examples of the Galatian church would be highly authoritarian churches or highly ritualized churches, highly legalistic churches. To my mind, these churches are the most obvious of the three examples we've

looked at, and therefore less dangerous. The first and second are much more prevalent, and perilous.

Is our Gospel the True Gospel?

Since the one true gospel is so crucial, and so often and easily reversed, this awakens in us a troubling question: how can we ensure the gospel *we* believe is actually true? How do we know it is not merely a gospel that we *feel* is true, or are *told* is true, or *think* is true, or *sounds* to us as true—but a gospel that *is* true, objectively, and therefore *can* save, really and eternally?

Paul lays down, in the strongest possible language, a plumb line for judging all truth claims, whether external (from teachers, writers, thinkers, preachers) or internal (feelings, sensations, experience). That standard is the gospel that he (and all the other capital-A Apostles) received from Christ and taught, and which is found in this letter and throughout the rest of the Bible.

"If we ... should preach a gospel other than the one ... let him be eternally condemned" (**v 8**). Here is how to judge external authorities such as human teachers, or human institutional leaders, or even ordained officers in a church hierarchy.

It is remarkable that by saying "we", Paul includes himself as a human authority. He is saying that *he* must be rejected if he ever says: *I've changed my mind about what the gospel is.* As he'll tell us, the gospel did not come to him through a process of reasoning and reflection; it was received, not arrived at. So he is not free to alter it through reasoning and reflecting. In Galatians 2, Paul will tell us that his gospel was confirmed by others who had also gotten the message by revelation from the risen Christ. This apostolic consensus—this original Christ-given "gospel deposit"—is therefore the touchstone for judging all truth claims, from the outside and the inside.

This is very important. Paul is saying in **verse 8** that even his apostolic authority derives from the gospel's authority, not the other way around. Paul is telling the Galatians to evaluate and judge both him as an apostle and his teaching with the biblical gospel. The Bible judges the church; the church does not judge the Bible. The Bible is the foundation for and the creator of the church; the church is not the foundation for or creator of the Bible. The church and its hierarchy must be evaluated by the believer with the biblical gospel as the touchstone or plumb line for judging all truth claims.

Nor is the final plumb line for truth our personal experience. We do not judge the Bible by our feelings or convictions; we judge our experiences by the Bible. That means that if an angel literally showed up before a crowd of people and taught that salvation was by good works (or anything except faith alone in Christ alone), you should literally kick the angel out (**v 8**)! When Paul says: "If we or an angel…," he gives a sweeping summary of proper Christian "epistemology"— how we know what is true.

Why it Matters

We noticed at the start of this chapter that Paul's tone is uncompromising, to say the least! But that's because the gospel is something we need to be uncompromising about. That's because, first, a different gospel means *you are deserting the one who called you (***v 6***)*. To abandon gospel **theology** is to abandon Christ personally. What you do in theology eventually affects your experience. In other words, a difference in your understanding of **doctrine** leads to a difference in your understanding of who Jesus is—and means it's questionable whether you really know Him at all.

Second, *a different gospel is no gospel at all* (**v 6b-7**). This means that the gospel message, by its very nature, cannot be changed even slightly without being lost. It's like a vacuum. You can't allow in some air and say that it is now a "90 per cent vacuum" or an "air-enriched vacuum". It is either a complete vacuum or no vacuum at all! Equally, the message of the gospel is that you are saved by grace through Christ's work and nothing else at all. As soon as you add anything to it, you have lost it entirely. The moment you revise it, you reverse it.

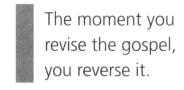

The moment you revise the gospel, you reverse it.

Third, *a different gospel brings condemnation (v 8-9)*. Later in the book Paul says that different "gospels" bring a curse with them. This means, ultimately, that to alter the gospel is to play with eternal life and death. But it also means very practically that fear, anxiety and guilt (the sense of condemnation and curse) will always be attached to different "gospels" even in this life. As we will see later in the book, even Christians sometimes experience a sense of condemnation. When they do, it is because, functionally, they are trusting in different "gospels", different ways to earn salvation. The "present evil age" (**v 4**) can still influence believers.

Now we can see why Paul adopts such intense and even severe language. The stakes are high—our knowledge of Christ, the truth of the gospel, and the eternal destiny of people's souls. These are things worth fighting for; worth speaking out over; worth reminding ourselves and others of over and over again. Paul's bluntness is loving. He is a capital-A Apostle who loves the Lord, the Lord's gospel, and the Lord's people. If we love as he did, we'll understand why he wrote as he did—and be grateful that he did.

Questions for reflection

1. How important is gospel truth to you? How is this shown in your life?

2. Why will understanding the true gospel produce anger at false "gospels"?

3. Which of the three modern false-gospel dangers could you or your church most easily fall for?

2. GOD'S AMAZING GRACE

Churches often ask members to share their **testimony** in a service or prayer meeting, and here we find the apostle Paul sharing his. In fact, Galatians 1:10 – 2:21 is often called the autobiographical section of the **epistle**, since Paul is recounting his conversion and early Christian experience. This is not a rare thing for Paul; we find him talking about his own conversion and experience in Acts 22:2b-21 and 26:4-23. And here, as in Acts, Paul is not sharing his testimony for general inspiration, or to point us to himself. He's using it to refute the claims of people who want to undermine his message, and he wants it all to point to the God of amazing grace.

Counter Claims

As Paul tells us how he became a follower of Jesus—or, perhaps more accurately, how Jesus made him His follower—he's defending himself from three attacks "some people" (v 7) were making on him and his gospel message.

First, Paul refutes the idea that he came to his gospel message through *his own reflection, reasoning and thinking*. He recounts that, until his conversion, he was "intensely" hostile to the church and to Christianity (**v 13**). He wanted to "destroy it". There was no gradual process of consideration, discussion, revision. There was no way that Paul's Christian message was the product of his own line of thinking. Rather, it was the exact, polar opposite of where he had been going.

Pre-Christian Paul was so violently opposed to Christ that even watching the faith and certainty of Christian martyrs had no effect on him (Acts 7:54 – 8:1). His experience is strong evidence that his conversion was via direct revelation. As Acts 9:1-9 shows us, the risen Jesus met and instructed Paul directly. Paul did not have simply a trance or a dream. Christ was there in time and space, since even the other men with Paul recognized the presence (Acts 9:7). So Paul became a "capital-A" apostle, like those who were apostles before him (**Galatians 1:17**).

> Paul did not have a dream. Christ was there in time and space.

Second, Paul undermines the claim that his gospel message was *derived from others, from Christian leaders* in **Jerusalem**. "I did not consult any man, nor did I go up to Jerusalem to see those who were apostles before I was" (**v 16-17**). There were three years between Paul's conversion and his first journey to Jerusalem (**v 18-19**), and even then he did not get instructed by them in any methodical way.

Paul's repeated reference to the apostles at Jerusalem suggest that "some people" (**v 7**) were claiming that Paul had simply gotten his gospel message from this "headquarters". This would enable them to argue: *We have also been trained at the Jerusalem HQ. And we know that Paul did not give you the whole story. There are other things you must do in order to be pleasing to God.*

Third, Paul shows that *his God-given gospel "checked out" with the message the other apostles had received from God.* Peter (**v 18**), James (**v 19**) and the churches of Judea (**v 22**) were among those who "praised God" (**v 24**) for what He had done for Paul, and for the message He had given Paul. He did not receive his commission or message from the other apostles; but his message squared with the one the other apostles received from the risen Lord (Luke 24:45-49).

So Paul's account eliminates claims like: *That's what Paul thinks—here's what we think, and it's just as valid; Paul's message is fine, but* incomplete; Paul's message is simply his message—it's not what the church teaches in Jerusalem.

But Paul's testimony doesn't only establish his authority as a gospel teacher. It also illustrates some aspects of what the gospel of grace *is*. You might think: *We covered this in Chapter One of this book!* And we did—but this letter, in its structure as well as its content, shows us that the gospel of grace underpins every step of the Christian life. Paul will keep coming back to it; so should we, in our lives, our prayers, our thoughts, our witness, our preaching and teaching.

Amazing Grace: Who Paul Was

Paul was a man who had done many terrible things. He had "intensely … persecuted the church of God and tried to destroy it" (**v 13**). By the time Jesus met Paul on the **Damascus road**, he had killed many innocent people. He was on his way to arrest and imprison more. He was filled with hate.

And yet Paul was also a man who had done many religious deeds. He had spent years seeking to live according to the Jewish customs and traditions. He says that he had beaten almost everyone of his own generation ("of my own age", **v 14**) at being **zealous** for moral righteousness (**v 14**). And yet it had not made him right with God.

Up until this point in the book, we have not been told the nature of the teaching of "some people" who were "trying to pervert the gospel" (**v 7**), but here is the first hint. Later we will see that they were encouraging the Gentile Christians to become full converts to Judaism, and to keep all the Mosaic laws of diet and dress, including **circumcision** (2:12; 3:5; 6:12). But Paul is saying: *I've already been there and done that! I know all about this subject! You cannot make yourself acceptable to God by the most zealous and detailed following of moral, ethical, or cultural codes.*

Before conversion, Paul was a great religious rule-keeper—and he knew it. He was filled with pride. And yet, despite all this, he was not only saved by Christ, but also called to be a preacher and leader of the faith. His testimony is a powerful witness to the beating heart of Christianity—the gospel of grace.

Grace is the free, unmerited favor of God, working powerfully on the mind and heart to change lives. There is no clearer example than Paul that salvation is by grace alone, not through our moral and religious performance. Though Paul's sins were very deep, he was invited in.

Paul's experience proves vividly that the gospel is not simply "religion" as it is generally understood. The gospel calls us out of *religion* as much as it calls us out of *irreligion*.

No one is so good that they don't need the grace of the gospel, nor so bad that they can't receive the grace of the gospel. Paul was deeply religious, but he needed the gospel. Paul was deeply flawed, yet he could be reached with the gospel. As C.S. Lewis once said: "Christianity must be from God, for who else could have thought it up?"

Amazing Grace: What God was Doing

As he looks back, Paul can now recognize that God's **sovereign** grace was working in his life long before his actual conversion. When Paul says God "set me apart from birth," (**v 15**) he means that the grace of God had been shaping and preparing him all his life for the things God was going to call him to do.

This is astonishing. Paul had been resisting God and doing so much wrong (see Acts 26:14), but God was overruling all his intentions and using his experiences and even his failures to prepare him first for his conversion, and then to be a preacher to the **Gentiles** (**v 16**). The Old Testament knowledge; the zeal; the training; the effort he was using to oppose God and His church (**v 13**)—all were being used by God to break him and to equip him to be God's instrument for building His church. God had been working all along to use Paul to establish the very faith he had opposed (**v 23**).

This is a major theme in the Bible. Back in Genesis, Joseph told his brothers that their very effort to reject him as God's chosen deliverer—in which they had gone so far as to try to kill him, and had then successfully sold him as a slave (Genesis 37:5-8, 19-20)—had actually been the means to establish Joseph *as* that deliverer (Genesis 50:19-20). The apostles insisted that the people who tried to oppose Jesus only served to further God's purposes (Acts 2:23; 4:27-28). All opposition to God will be seen in the end as having done nothing but confirm and further His design.

In chapter 9 of his spiritual autobiography, *Surprised by Joy*, C.S. Lewis tells of his school teacher, Kirkpatrick. Nicknamed "The Great Knock", he was a furious debater and logician who taught Lewis how to build a case and make strong arguments. Kirkpatrick was an atheist, and

> All opposition will be seen in the end as having done nothing but further God's design.

he intended to strengthen Lewis in his own unbelief. But years later, when Lewis became a Christian, it turned out that "The Great Knock" had trained him well to become one of the greatest defenders of the Christian faith in the 20th century.

The gospel gives us a pair of spectacles through which we can review our own lives and see God preparing us and shaping us, even through our own failures and sins, to become vessels of His grace in the world.

So why did all this happen? Why did God choose, prepare and then call Paul, the proud persecutor of His church? Was it because Paul was in some way, in any way, pleasing to God? No, it was simply because God "was pleased" to do so (**v 15**). God set His loving grace on Paul not because he was worthy of it, but simply because God took delight or pleasure in doing so. This is how God has always worked. As Moses tells God's people Israel in Deuteronomy 7:7-8: "The LORD did not set his affection on you and choose you because you were more numerous than other peoples, for you were the fewest of all peoples. But *it was because the LORD loved you.*"

God does not love us because we are serviceable; He loves us simply because He loves us. This is the only kind of love we can ever be secure in, of course, since it is the only kind of love we cannot possibly lose. This is grace.

Questions for reflection

1. Do you ever find yourself thinking you deserve God's grace? What prompts you to think this way?

2. How does the gospel of grace free you from pride and from guilt?

3. In what ways can you see how God worked in your life before your conversion, to equip you to serve Him after it?

PART TWO

Amazing Grace: What God is Doing

The God of grace saves sinners like Paul. He reveals His risen Son to both the proud and the evil—the religious and the irreligious. And He's at work in His people even before He saves them, to bring them to faith and to equip them to serve Him.

But that is not where grace finishes its work. Grace has continued to work in and through Paul. The apostle testifies not only of who he was, and of how God converted him, but also of what a life lived under God's grace looks like.

First, we read that God was pleased "to reveal his Son in me, so that I might preach" (**v 16**). What Paul means here is not immediately clear. What does it mean that God revealed Jesus "in" Paul? The best interpretation is that Paul is combining two experiences in one. On the one hand, God obviously revealed Jesus to Paul on the road to Damascus. There Paul finally realized who Jesus was. He had a personal encounter with the living Christ. But secondly (as the rest of **v 16** shows), Paul immediately realized that he was being called to show others who Jesus was. So we can say that God revealed Christ *to* Paul so that He could reveal Christ *through* Paul.

This shows us a critical difference between a mere religious or moral person, and a *Christian*. A Christian has more than an intellectual belief in Christ; they sense a personal relationship. And they know that this relationship is not given to them solely for their own personal comfort and joy. They know they have a responsibility to reveal Christ to others through what they are, do, and say.

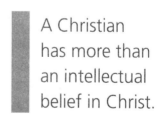

A Christian has more than an intellectual belief in Christ.

Second, we see something of Paul's own path of growth and discipleship. He had solitary time with God. During his three years in **Arabia** (**v 17-18**), we assume he learned from God much that he later taught. Though we should not think that his time in Arabia was spent simply in solitude (there were thriving cities there), we do learn about the importance of study and reflection and the development of our own personal acquaintance with God. We live in a time that puts too much emphasis on activity and accomplishment, and not enough on reflection and contemplation.

(This reference to Arabia is unique in the New Testament. And if we press the word "immediately" (**v 17**) too literally, it seems to conflict with Acts 9:19-22, where Paul did some synagogue preaching immediately after his baptism. But Paul's point here is that he went to Arabia, rather than Jerusalem, for his first sustained time of reflection and preparation.)

Solitary time with God is fundamental to the Christian life; but the Christian life is not a solitary one. Paul went up to Jerusalem not for instruction, but for both accountability and unity (**v 18**). Even Paul must work on unity with the other apostles and must demonstrate that his message squares with theirs. How much more do we have the same responsibility? We too must be deeply rooted in church communities. We have to avoid picking what we need here and there without ever becoming grafted into a cohesive community of other believers.

Such a Christian life, rooted in relationship with God through Christ, and in unity with and service of other believers, leads to praise of God. The Christians in Jerusalem "praised God because of me," says Paul (**v 24**). The change in Paul's life and his service to others did not lead people to lionize Paul, but to love God.

Amazing Grace: How it Changes Us

This whole section of Paul's testimony is introduced by **verse 10**: "Am I now trying to win the approval of men, or of God?" Paul asks. It's a question with an obvious answer: God!

The gospel removes a "man-pleasing" spirit—the drive to "win the approval of men". It replaces that spirit with its opposite—not needing to win or seek human approval for what you do. In other words, the gospel produces confident and fearless followers of Jesus, doing what is right without concern for the approval and good opinion of others. Paul says that he *couldn't* be a "servant of Christ" if he were a people-pleaser.

That is to say, a Christian *cannot* and *will not* be a man-pleaser. This certainly underscores its importance!

The Bible talks about the sin of man-pleasing under a number of different headings and phrases. When you put them all together, there is a surprising amount of material on it. Proverbs 29:25 says: "Fear of man will prove to be a snare". This fear of people is the opposite of "fear of God". In the Old Testament, the fear of God does not simply mean to be frightened by Him, but to be filled with awe and wonder and attraction at His greatness. Therefore, the "fear of man" must refer to a view of people (or a particular person or group of people) that causes you to elevate their importance, to hold them in awe, to crave their approval and to fear their disapproval. It is a situation in which your desire for their blessing amounts to adoration and worship, and in which you give some form of human approval the rights and power over your heart that only God should have. It means you will be as devastated by the loss of this approval as if you felt criticized or condemned by God.

> Fear of man means that your desire for their blessing amounts to worship.

The fear of man presents itself in many ways. When Saul disobeyed God in 1 Samuel 15:24, it was because he was afraid of public opinion. When Samson gave in to Delilah (Judges 16), it was because he was afraid of losing her sexual attention.

Elsewhere, Paul mentions another very common form—what we might call eye-service (Ephesians 6:6-7; Colossians 3:22-23). It means to do a job only to the degree that you get approval of, or reward from, those over you. If you work that way, you will do inconsistent, shoddy, and half-hearted work. You will never create anything for the excellence and joy of creation and a job well done.

So, how does the gospel destroy man-pleasing—"the fear of man"? By freeing us and motivating us to seek "to win the approval of ... God" (**v 10**). In the gospel, we discover that trusting in Christ brings God's full and complete favor and approval. When He sees the believer, He sees Jesus (3:25-27)—and so He says to us: "With you I am well pleased" (Mark 1:11). God is pleased with us.

And because God is pleased with us, we can live in a way which pleases God, the Creator of the cosmos. Paul seeks to please God, rather than people (v 10). He urges Christians to sacrificially obey God because this is "pleasing to God" (Romans 12:1).

Imagine a father watching his beloved son play baseball for the team his father coaches. As he sits in the dugout, he loves his son fully and completely. If his son forgets his father's instructions and strikes out, it will not change his love for him or approval of him one bit. The son is assured of his father's love regardless of his performance.

But the son will long to hit that home run. Not for himself—to gain his father's love—but for his father, because he is already loved. If he doesn't know his father loves him, his efforts will be for himself—to win that love. Because he knows his father already loves him, his efforts are for his father—to please him.

The Christian is assured of God's love and approval. God is pleased with us in Christ. So the Christian longs to obey God, not for himself, so that God will save him, but out of gratitude to God, who he knows has already saved him. And so Paul lives as a "servant of Christ" (v 10). God's approval liberates us to live in a way which God approves of. The gospel is both a powerful assurance, and a powerful motivation to live in radical

> God's approval liberates us to live in a way which God approves of.

obedience. We do not live God's way in order to become His children, but out of gratitude that we are already God's children.

Paul's Testimony, and Ours

Paul does not share his testimony out of habit, nor for general inspirational purposes, nor because he enjoys putting a spotlight on his personal experiences. He only shares his testimony because he believes it will help his hearers find Christ, and encourage them not to lose Him (**v 6**). He has no desire for attention or acclaim. He is completely focused on his listeners. He is not using his hearers to boost his ego, but using his testimony to help his friends.

Paul is a good example to us here. He shows us that we must have the courage to be vulnerable and speak personally about what the gospel means to us. Why? Because Christianity is an appeal to bring our whole life, mind and heart, to Christ. To leave out how we think, or how we feel, is to give an incomplete picture of how comprehensive Christian commitment is. If we leave out our testimony, it also gives an incomplete picture of how complete Christian fulfillment is. Christ not only appeals to our minds, he fills our hearts. Different cultures and personalities have different emphases on the cognitive (head-understanding) and the experiential (heart-feeling). If you leave out your testimony, the more

> Christ not only appeals to our minds, he fills our hearts.

heart-focused cultures and temperaments will not see the attractiveness of Christianity.

At the same time, Paul also reminds us that we must only share our testimony if it is helpful to others. Strange as it may sound, it is very easy to use our testimony in a way that clouds the gospel.

If we emphasize dramatic, gory, or sexual details, we may only be sending the message: *Look at what an amazing case I am!* Paul gets personal only to make the gospel clear. We are not sharing our story for ourselves, but to help others understand and find Christ; to point others to the amazing gospel of grace which has changed our lives, and which we know can change theirs, too.

Questions for reflection

1. How could you live your life so that people would respect and praise God more because of you?

2. How are you most tempted to fear men and seek their approval? What would change if, in those moments, you lived to please the God who is pleased with you?

3. How committed are you to spending time with God... to spending time with other believers... to spending time telling others your testimony?

3. GOSPEL UNITY

We should read this passage with great fear and gratitude. It takes us to a meeting in Jerusalem which may seem distant from the concerns of 21st-century Christians. But in fact, the stakes could not have been higher—it was a meeting which had huge consequences for us all, even today. And, as we'll see, God protected all of us—you and me—on that day.

Paul's Fear: Why he went

Paul, still writing autobiographically, moves us on to a time "fourteen years later" than his first visit to Jerusalem, when he "went up again", along with two trusted members of his mission team, Barnabas and Titus (**v 1**).

Why did he go? "In response to a revelation" from God externally, and "for fear" internally (**v 2**). This should make us pause. The Paul who we meet in Acts and his letters isn't a man given to feeling afraid! First, he was a bold persecutor of the church; then, he was a still bolder preacher of the gospel. So why was a man such as this afraid?

At first glance, it might seem that Paul was concerned that he had been wrong in his message or in his methods, and so he went back to Jerusalem to meet with the other apostles "privately" to "set before [the leaders] the gospel that I preach" (**v 2**), to get confirmation that he was doing things correctly. But that is impossible for several reasons.

First, Paul went to Jerusalem "in response to a revelation" from God (**v 2**). This reminds us that he was an apostle with direct access to God. He had received his gospel from the lips of the visible, risen

Christ (1:12). It makes no sense for someone getting revelations from God to go and get authorization from someone else! Second, if he had been uncertain, why wait 14 years before heading back to Jerusalem? And third, Paul said in 1:8 that the Galatians should reject even Paul himself ("we") if he should come and say he'd changed his mind about the gospel.

Nothing was threatening Paul's *certainty*, but something was threatening his *fruitfulness*.

If the other apostles did not confirm his message and renounce the false teachers, it would be very hard for him to retain his converts. False teachers were telling these young Christians that Paul was preaching a gospel that was inadequate and not as full as the original apostolic gospel preached by the Jerusalem leaders. They insisted that Paul taught an "easy believism" that was his own very eccentric message.

Paul knew his message was God-revealed and therefore true. But he would not be able to keep his churches in sound gospel teaching if he could not disprove this falsehood. That is why Paul feared he was in danger of "running [his] race in vain" (**v 2**). He was afraid that his ministry would be stifled and relatively fruitless.

Equally, Paul's trip was not "for fear" that the Jerusalem apostles didn't have the true gospel. What he did fear was that the Jerusalem apostles might not be true to that gospel. They might not stand up to the false teachers, but rather, allow their own cultural prejudices to entice them to let these teachers continue to make such damaging claims.

The Stakes: True Church Unity

On the one side of this dispute we have Paul, who is saying: *The gospel of faith in Christ is for people of all cultures*. On the other we have his opponents, claiming: *Not all Jewish people are Christians, but all Christians must become Jewish.*

If the Jerusalem apostles had sided with, or even merely tolerated, those who were teaching against Paul, this would have split the church in two. Neither side would have accepted the other fully, and would have questioned if the others were saved! Paul's Gentile churches would doubt that the Jewish churches really had faith in Christ, and the Jewish churches would also doubt the salvation of the Gentiles.

John Stott put it this way:

> "It was one thing for the Jerusalem leaders to give their approval to the conversion of the Gentiles, but could they approve of ... commitment to the Messiah without inclusion in Judaism?
> Was their vision big enough to see the gospel of Christ not as a reform movement within Judaism but as good news for the whole world, and the church of Christ ... as the international family of God?" *(The Message of Acts,* page 241)

The other apostles had stayed in Jerusalem, and they had not worked out the implications of the gospel for Gentiles who were converting from paganism. They simply had not confronted most of these issues practically. It would have been extremely easy for them to miss the implications of the gospel when it came to living as a Gentile Christian. It would have felt natural for them to say: *Of course all Christians should eat **kosher**!* or something similar. But the ramifications of such a "small" mistake would have been enormous. There would have been two opposing parties within Christianity that were hostile to each other on the fundamental point of whether we need to add external behaviors to internal belief in Christ in order to be saved.

> The ramifications of such a "small" mistake would have been enormous.

That's why Paul said that "the freedom we have in Christ" (**v 4**) was under threat, and therefore that the very "truth of the gospel" was at stake (**v 5**). This meeting could have ended up splitting the church; and at such an early stage in its life, two virtually different religions would have emerged. No wonder Paul felt fear. The stakes could not have been higher.

The Verdict: Welcome

It was crucial that Paul "took Titus along also" (**v 1**). Titus "was a Greek" (**v 3**)—a flesh-and-blood, uncircumcised Christian. Paul's "false brothers" (**v 4**) who had "infiltrated our ranks"—the church—would have insisted that, in order to be saved, Titus needed to trust Christ *and* live according to Jewish rituals, such as circumcision. So in Titus, Paul confronted the other apostles with a concrete test case. The Jerusalem meeting could not be an abstract discussion. Would they require Titus to be circumcised, or not?

> Titus was a test case. Would the apostles require him to be circumcised?

"Yet not even Titus, who was with me, was compelled to be circumcised, even though he was a Greek" (**v 3**). By God's grace, the Jerusalem apostles rose to the occasion and "walked the walk" rather than just "talking the talk". They did not insist on Titus' circumcision before having fellowship with him. "God does not judge by external appearance" (**v 6**). Externalities are to do with our doing; internalities have to do with our being; and Christianity is about who I am in Christ, not what I do for Him.

Paul says "they added nothing to my message" (**v 6**). The Jerusalem apostles agreed that it is faith in Christ alone, and not any other performance or ritual, that is necessary for salvation. Their acceptance of Titus was proof that they had accepted Paul's ministry and these radical implications of the gospel.

The implications of this are fundamental to our understanding of what the Christian faith is. The countless regulations for "cleanliness" in the laws of Moses were designed (among other things) to show us how impossible it was to make ourselves perfectly acceptable before a holy God. But these "false brothers" had used the regulations in order to teach the exact opposite: that we could make ourselves pure and more acceptable to God through strict compliance with them.

The number of times the New Testament talks about this mistake shows how easy it is to get it wrong. "The gifts and sacrifices being offered were not able to clear the conscience of the worshiper. They are only a matter of food and drink and various ceremonial washings—external regulations applying until the time of the new order" (Hebrews 9:9-10; see also Colossians 2:16). Only in Christ can we become "**holy** in his sight, without blemish and free from accusation" (Colossians 1:22). In other words, these ceremonial laws have not been so much abolished or replaced as fulfilled. They are fulfilled in Christ; it is Christ who makes us clean (see Mark 7:14-19; John 13:2-11).

So the acceptance of Titus by Jewish believers was a vivid illustration of this principle, that an individual becomes spiritually clean and acceptable through Christ, and not through any deeds or rituals. We need to keep repeating this truth to ourselves and each other, just as the New Testament did. Gentiles could become full members of the people of God without becoming Jewish in custom or culture. The acceptance of Titus was a radical public statement of the implications of the gospel.

The Outcome: Freedom

In **verse 4**, Paul characterizes the two sides of this argument in an illuminating way. The "false brothers" who had infiltrated the Gentile churches wanted, he says, "to make us slaves", preventing them from enjoying "the freedom we have in Christ Jesus". Paul is saying that the biblical gospel gives freedom, while his opponents' "earn-your-salvation" message would lead people only into slavery.

This is a theme he'll return to throughout his letter (especially in 4:21-31). So how does the gospel give freedom?

First, the gospel leads to *cultural* freedom. Moralistic religion tends to press its members to adopt very specific rules and regulations for dress and daily behavior. Why? If your salvation depends upon obeying the rules, then you want your rules to be very specific, do-able and clear. You don't want: *Love your neighbor as yourself*, because that's an impossibly high standard which has endless implications! You want: *Don't go to movies* or *Don't drink alcohol* or *Don't eat this type of food*.

> If salvation depends upon obeying rules, you want your rules to be specific and do-able.

But rules and regulations like this get into the area of daily cultural life. If the false teachers had had their way, an Italian or African could not become a Christian without becoming culturally Jewish. Christians would have to form little cultural ghettoes in every city. It would mean far too much emphasis on external cultural separation rather than on internal distinctiveness of spirit, motive, outlook and perspective. Elevating cultural propriety to the level of spiritual virtue leads Christians to a slavish emphasis on being culturally "nice" and "proper", as well as promoting intolerant and prejudiced attitudes.

Second, the gospel leads to *emotional* freedom. Anyone who believes that our relationship with God is based on keeping up moral behavior is on an endless treadmill of guilt and insecurity. As we know from Paul's letters, he did not free Gentile believers from the moral imperatives of the Ten Commandments. Christians could not lie, steal, commit adultery and so on. But though not free from the moral law as *a way to live,* Christians are free from the it as a *system of salvation*. We obey not in the fear and insecurity of hoping to earn our salvation, but in the freedom and security of knowing we are already saved in Christ. We obey in the freedom of gratitude.

So both the false teachers and Paul told Christians to obey the Ten Commandments, but for totally different reasons and motives. And unless your motive for obeying God's law is the grace-gratitude motive of the gospel, you are in slavery. The gospel provides freedom, culturally and emotionally. The "other gospel" destroys both.

Questions for reflection

1. Have there been times in your life when you have begun to think that your performance counts toward your salvation? What caused you to think this way?

2. What are the "nice" and "proper" attitudes that your culture and upbringing has taught you? How could you add these on to belief in Christ as an expectation for other Christians?

3. Do you ever feel guilty or insecure in your relationship with God? What might this be telling you about how you view your acceptance with Him?

PART TWO

Two Marks of Real Unity

It is very easy, in an age of fractured churches and **denominational** bickering, to miss the repeated emphasis that the New Testament places on Christian unity. So, what does real Christian unity look like?

First, as we have seen, it means accepting anyone and everyone who is "in Christ Jesus" (**v 4**), regardless of their cultural and ethnic background. An American Christian has far more in common with a gospel-believer who lives a nomadic existence on the Mongolian plains than they do with a non-believer who lives on their street, drives a similar car, and whose children go to the same school as theirs. Christian unity takes no account of cultural distinctives and is never contingent on cultural similarity.

> Christian unity takes no account of cultural distinctives.

So, just as Titus was not "compelled to be circumcised" (**v 3**), so today we must not insist on additions to gospel belief. Some churches teach that we must believe in Christ plus be baptized in order to be saved. Others insist that we must belong to their church in order to be saved. Many types of Christianity add their distinctions, such as belief in **predestination**, abstinence from alcohol or **speaking in tongues**, to the gospel as ways we can be sure we are Christians. In other words, many churches will say that we are saved by faith alone, but we can only be sure that we are real Christians if we have these distinctions. Many churches and Christian groups add cultural rules— about things like dress and amusements—to the Bible, and insist that no one who violates these standards could possibly be a Christian.

Second, it means recognizing that we have different callings. The apostles recognized this within their own number: "they saw that I had been entrusted with the task of preaching the gospel to the Gentiles, as Peter had been to the Jews" (**v 7**). Though Peter and Paul were preaching "the [same] gospel", they recognized that there are different ways to go about it. Some people have a gift and ability to communicate the gospel to one group of people, and others to a different group.

The implication of this is that we can adapt the gospel to different people while preserving its essence. This is an important implication for mission. If we fail to adapt the gospel message at all to the interests of people, or if we over-adapt it and lose its essence, we will fail to persuade and win people into its joy and freedom.

What are common ways in which we might fail to preserve the message today? Some churches and Christians have adapted the gospel to the modern world by removing "offensive" elements like miracles of any sort or the demand that we can only come to God through Christ. But then the gospel itself is gone, since we are left in a position of having to save ourselves by being good. That is a failure to preserve.

On the other hand, it is possible to go too far in the other direction, and fail to adapt. Many churches and Christians are so wedded to their music or organization or jargon that they are not willing to make changes to incorporate the tastes and sensibilities of outsiders.

Ironically, if you under-adapt *or* over-adapt, you "lose" the gospel. If you raise your traditions to the place of non-negotiables, you essentially create a system of **legalism**. You are saying: *Real Christians always do things this way*. So both conservatism and legalism (non-adaptation) can threaten the gospel just as much as liberalism (non-preservation) does. The apostles were determined to preserve the gospel message, and the lifestyle implications of it; but they were equally prepared to adapt the medium of that message.

> If you raise your traditions to the place of non-negotiables, you essentially create legalism.

A Challenging Third Mark

Third, and perhaps surprisingly, Christian unity means "we should continue to remember the poor" (**v 10**). Peter and Paul may have been called to different mission fields, but they were both constrained to look after the poor. The Jerusalem apostles wanted to insist on this, and they met a willing worker in Paul, who was "eager" to do this anyway (v 10). Why is remembering the poor fundamental to Christian unity?

There are two reasons: a general one, and a particular one. The *particular* reason in the context of this Jerusalem meeting was that the Jewish churches were much poorer than the churches Paul was planting in Gentile areas. Donald Guthrie puts it this way:

> "The condition of the Judean Christians ... their poverty called
> forth the sympathy of the Gentile churches (see Romans
> 15:25-28; 1 Corinthians 16:1-4; 2 Corinthians 8 – 9)."
>
> (*Galatians*, page 83)

The Jerusalem apostles were therefore urging that the Gentile and Jewish churches stay tightly interconnected, sharing their resources with each other just as they were shared within the local congregation (Acts 4:32).

The *general* reason is that care for the poor is a constant in the Bible. Here is a (very condensed!) summary of biblical teaching about it.

Jesus proves to **John the Baptist** that He is the Christ by pointing out that He heals bodies and preaches to the poor (Matthew 11:1-6), even as the **prophets** said He would (Isaiah 11:1-4; 61:1-2). Jesus teaches that anyone who has truly been touched by the grace of a merciful God will be vigorous in helping the needy (as implied by Luke 6:35- 36; Matthew 5:43-48). God will judge whether or not we have justifying faith by looking at our service to the poor, the refugee, the sick and the prisoner (Matthew 25:44-46).

Jesus, of course, provided the perfect example of this. In His **incarnation**, He "moved in" with the poor (Luke 2:24; 2 Corinthians 8:9). He lived, ate, and associated with the lowest class of society. He called this "mercy" (Matthew 9:13). The Bible demands that we emulate him (2 Corinthians 8:8-15). Christians are to open their hands to the needy as far as there is need (1 John 3:16-17; see Deuteronomy 15:7-8), and within the church, wealth is to be shared very generously between rich and poor (2 Corinthians 8:13-15; see Leviticus 25). Echoing the prophets, the apostles teach that true faith will inevitably show itself through deeds of mercy (James 2:1-23). Materialism is still a grievous sin (James 5:1-6; 1 Timothy 6:17-19).

Not only do all believers have these responsibilities, but also a special class of officers—deacons—are established to coordinate the church's ministry of mercy (Acts 6:1-7). This shows that the ministry of mercy is a required, mandated work of the church just as the ministry of the word and discipline are (Romans 15:23-29). Paul tells the Ephesian elders in his farewell address that he has taught them the whole counsel of God (Acts 20:27). It is highly significant, then, that in his very last words, Paul exhorts them to give to the weak and poor (v 35). Not only did Paul consider mercy to the poor as part of the whole counsel of God, but he also deemed it so crucial as to make it the very last piece of encouragement he gave them—as did the Jerusalem apostles to him in **Galatians 2:10**. Christians are to be united by, and in, a care for the poor.

The Limits of Unity

We can easily make far too little of Christian unity today, focusing on what divides us from fellow believers in the gospel rather than on the Lord and Savior who has brought us together. But the opposite error is equally dangerous: making too much of unity at the expense of it being Christian.

Remember, "this matter"—the whole point of Paul's trip to Jerusalem—"arose because some false brothers had infiltrated" the church (**v 4**). The meeting only happened because Paul was not willing to share a church with those who taught a different gospel. The relationship of co-operation between the apostles was based on *shared gospel truth*. Paul and his companions all received "the right hand of fellowship" from the Jerusalem leaders (**v 9**). "Giving the right hand" was just as much a sign of friendship, co-operation, and approval in the ancient world as it is today. This was more than a gesture of courtesy. This act had the effect of isolating and discrediting the false teachers. They could no longer claim to represent James, Peter, and John (as they evidently had, 2:12). By including Paul, Barnabas and the uncircumcised Titus, the Jerusalem apostles were excluding the false teachers. By establishing gospel unity, they were also setting the boundaries of that unity—and the "false brothers" were outside it.

Fellowship with Christ is a sufficient basis for fellowship with one another. We must never exclude someone whom God has included in His people. But equally, fellowship with Christ is the *only* basis for fellowship with one another. Churches must not maintain unity at the expense of the gospel.

Freedom and community are two great yearnings of the human heart. Neither longing is ultimately satisfied by any worldview or religion which is based on "earn-your-salvation" **tenets**. These will divide people on cultural lines, and enslave them emotionally. It is "in Christ Jesus" that we can enjoy the freedom of acceptance by God regardless of our performance; and that we can enjoy a unity which pays no attention to countries' borders or cultural boundaries. It was this unity and this freedom that Paul's gospel offered; and it was in defense of these that God prompted him to go to Jerusalem two thousand years ago. Division and slavery were things Paul "did not give in to" (**v 5**)—neither should we!

> Freedom and community are two great yearnings of the human heart.

Questions for reflection

1. Can you think of examples of churches not prizing gospel unity sufficiently; or pursuing institutional unity at the expense of gospel truth?

2. How are you caring for the poor? How has Galatians 2:10 encouraged and/or challenged you?

3. Both personally and as part of your church, do you tend to over-adapt or under-adapt the gospel for the culture around you?

4. LIVING IN LINE WITH THE GOSPEL

Paul's visit to Jerusalem established the great, uniting truth that we are saved by faith in Christ; nothing else, and nothing more. Now he switches his focus from standing alongside Peter in Jerusalem, the capital of Israel, to standing against him in **Antioch**, a Gentile city. Both times, what matters to Paul more than anything is the gospel— the gospel which, in this passage, he summarizes for the first time in the letter as "justification by faith".

Table Manners

Verse 11 is astonishing; here we have two apostles meeting together, and one of them recalls that he "opposed" the other "to his face, because he was clearly in the wrong". What could cause two apostles to fall into such a position?

Paul explains the presenting issue simply. Peter had changed his eating habits: "He used to eat with the Gentiles … he began to draw back and separate himself from the Gentiles" (**v 12**).

To a first-century Jew, far more surprising than Peter *stopping* eating food with Gentiles would have been the fact that he had *started* eating with them in the first place.

The Old Testament instituted the "clean laws", a complicated series of regulations for worshippers to follow in order to be "ceremonially clean" and acceptable for the presence of God in worship. People could not draw near to God if they ate certain "unclean" foods, if they had touched dead things, if they had a disease or touched someone who did, and so on (see Leviticus 11; 15; 20). This "ceremonial" law was a teaching method by which the holy God showed that sinful people cannot go into His presence without cleansing. Despite Jesus explaining that with His arrival the time for these laws had passed (Mark 7:14-23), God had to send Peter a vision to show him why the ceremonial law was finished. He saw a great sheet full of animals forbidden for eating in the Old Testament, and he heard a voice saying: "Kill and eat … Do not call anything impure that God has made clean" (Acts 11:7, 9). Immediately, Peter meets a repentant Gentile, Cornelius, who receives Christ and is born again. Peter realizes: "God does not show favoritism but accepts men from every nation who fear him" (Acts 10:34-35).

Afterwards, he eats with Gentiles despite criticism (11:2). Even later, he argues that the Gentiles have been "purified [made clean] by faith" (15:7-9). Peter began eating with Gentiles because God had shown him that no one is "unclean" in Christ.

So when Peter withdrew from the Gentiles, he was guilty of "hypocrisy" (**Galatians 2:13**). He had not changed his convictions—he knew the food and dress laws were only "Jewish customs", and he didn't keep to all of them (**v 14**). But when it came to Gentiles, he had simply stopped acting in accord with those convictions. And this hypocrisy was infectious: "Even Barnabas [a mission partner of the uncircumcised Gentile Titus!] was led astray" (**v 13**).

> Peter had simply stopped acting in accord with his convictions.

What caused this hypocrisy? "He was afraid" (**v 12**). Likely, Peter was afraid of criticism from "those who belonged to the circumcision group"—which is Paul's way of describing "salvation-through-Christ-plus-something" teachers.

But in addition, racial pride must have entered into it. It had been drilled into Peter, and all the Jews, since their youth that Gentiles were "unclean". While hiding beneath the facade of religious observance, Peter and other Jewish Christians were probably still feeling disdain for Christians from "inferior" national and racial backgrounds. Peter was allowing cultural differences to become more important than gospel unity.

Straight-Walking

Paul does not primarily see his fellow apostle's behavior as rude, or unmannered, or unwelcoming, as we might. Fundamentally, he sees that something deeper is going on. Peter is "not acting in line with the truth of the gospel" (**v 14**).

Literally, Paul says that he was "not ortho-walking with the gospel". (The prefix *ortho* means to be straight—so we go to an ortho-dontist to straighten out our teeth.) This means, first, that the gospel is a truth—it is a message, a set of claims. It includes the fact that we are weak and sinful, that we seek to control our lives by being our own saviors and lords, that God's law was fulfilled by Christ for us, that we are now accepted completely though we are still very sinful and flawed, and so on.

And crucially it means, second, that this gospel truth has a vast number of implications for all of life. It is our job to bring everything in our lives "in line" with the thrust, or direction, of the gospel. We are to think out its implications in every area of our lives, and seek to bring our thinking, feeling, and behavior "in line".

The gospel "truth" is radically opposed to the assumptions of the world. But since we live in the world, we have embraced many of the world's assumptions. Christian living is therefore a continual realignment process—one of bringing everything in line with the truth of the gospel.

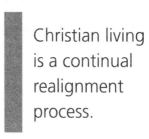 Christian living is a continual realignment process.

Peter's Mistake (and ours?)

Peter's sin was basically the sin of nationalism. He insisted that Christians can't be really pleasing to God unless they become Jewish. But nationalism is just one form of legalism. Legalism is looking to something besides Jesus Christ in order to be acceptable and clean before God. Legalism always results in pride and fear, psychologically, and exclusion and strife, socially.

There are many examples today of similar sorts of exclusive social behavior based on a failure to understand and live out justification by faith. Here are just a few.

One way is to be sectarian. Every Christian group or denomination necessarily has many distinctions of belief and practice that have less to do with the core gospel beliefs and more to do with specific convictions about ethical behavior or church policy. It is extremely easy to stress our distinctions in order to demonstrate to ourselves and others that our church is the superior or best one.

Another way is to bring class-ist, nationalistic, or racist attitudes from the world into the church. We all know Christians who belong to classes, groups, or personality types that we had previously disdained in our lives outside the church. Working-class Christians may have a distaste for Christians from wealthier or more socially "refined" backgrounds, and vice versa. Christians from one political persuasion may be upset by the presence of those from the other end of the spectrum. Very talented Christians may feel unhappy that people they consider mediocre are treated as equal parts of their church. Socially polished Christians feel uncomfortable around believers who are socially awkward or marginal (and vice versa).

We may feel uncomfortable around people whose cultural emphases are different to ours. And we may respond to all this as Peter did, in apparently well-mannered ways.

We politely sit by "those other people" in church, but we won't "eat" with them; we won't really become friends with them. We won't socialize with them, sharing our lives and homes and things with them. We will keep relationships formal and see them at official church meetings only.

All this comes from not living in line with the gospel. Without the gospel, our hearts have to manufacture self-esteem by comparing our group with other groups. But the gospel tells us we are all unclean without Christ, and all clean in Him.

> We politely sit by "those other people" in church, but we won't "eat" with them.

Lastly, the most subtle way to lapse into Peter's sin is simply to take our own preferences too seriously and endow with moral significance what is only cultural. For example, it is very hard for Christians from churches with emotional expressiveness and modern music not to feel superior to churches with emotional reserve and classical music, and vice versa. We cannot see that we are just different; we believe that our style and customs are spiritually better. This leads to all sorts of divisions in the body of Christ.

Paul's Response (and ours?)

Paul sees the principle behind Peter's changed eating practices. And in speaking to him about it, he points to the principle rather than simply aiming to change his behavior.

Paul's basic line is: God did not have fellowship with you on the basis of your race and culture (**v 15**). Though you were good and devout, your race and customs had nothing to do with it (**v 16**). Therefore, how can you have fellowship on the basis of race and culture (**v 14**)?

Paul does not simply say that racism is a sin, which it is. He uses the *gospel* to show Peter the spiritual roots of the mistake he's making. Paul says the roots of racism are a resistance to the gospel of salvation. In other words, racism is a continuation of works-righteousness in one part of our lives; it is born of a desire to find a way to feel we are in some way "better" or "righteous". It is forgetting that we are saved by grace; a failure to bring our relationships with other cultures in line with grace-salvation.

If you are a member of a racial majority, your race's cultural pride is fairly easy to see. If you are a member of a racial minority that is often put down, discernment of "justification-through-racial-pride" is a bit more complex. But it surfaces when you begin to think: *I'm more noble than you of the dominant race. I have suffered more and I'm not an oppressor like you.*

Paul's approach makes all the difference. Paul did not simply say: *You're breaking the rules* (even though Peter was), but: *You've forgotten the gospel: your own gracious welcome in Christ.* Paul did not focus so much on the sinful behavior as on the sinful attitude of self-righteousness that lay beneath it.

> Paul did not focus so much on the sinful behavior as on the sinful attitude.

This is the Christian way of "opposing" someone. When you are trying to motivate people by urging them to see their riches and love in Christ, then you personally are pointing to their value and dignity as you appeal. But when you try to motivate people by threatening them, you will probably feel little respect for them as you do so, and they will (rightly) sense that you are not on their side. When we use God's grace as a motivator, we can criticize sharply and directly, but the other person will generally be able to perceive that we are nonetheless for them. No wonder Paul was winsome in this situation!

Keep this in mind, too. Peter's racial pride was grounded in fear (**v 12**—he was afraid). When our sin is rooted in fear, we need to be loved and strengthened in order to get the courage to do right despite our fear. Not only was Peter's *racism* "out of line" with the gospel; his *cowardice* was, too. As we'll see, Peter is justified in God's eyes (v 15-16). So why does he need to be justified in anyone else's? If Paul had only said: *Your cultural superiority is a violation of the rules of God*, his cowardice would have remained unaddressed, dormant, ready to make itself known in a different way. But in reminding him that he is justified already, Paul is saying: *Peter, you don't need approval from these men. You've already got Christ's.*

We don't often remember to treat each other in this gospel-founded way. Christians tend to motivate others with guilt. We tend to say: *You would do this if you were really committed Christians*, indicating that we are committed and all that is needed is for others to become as good as we are! This is why so many churches quench the motivation of people for ministry. In our shoes, Paul would say: *Remember the grace God has showered on you—what does living out and enjoying that grace look like in this situation?*

Questions for reflection

1. In which areas have you been increasingly walking in line with the gospel over the last month? The last year?

2. Are there people in your church you have not been "eating with" because they are not "like you"? What self-righteousness lies beneath this attitude?

3. How could you motivate yourself, and other Christians, less with guilt and more with the gospel?

PART TWO

Justification by Faith

The climax of Paul's speech to Peter "in front of them all" (**v 14**) comes in **verse 16**: "We, too, have put our faith in Christ Jesus that we may be justified by faith in Christ and not by observing the law, because by observing the law no one will be justified".

"Justified by faith" is central to the Christian faith. It is Paul's nutshell summary of the gospel. But we often assume that we (and everyone else) have grasped what it means, and what impact it will have on our lives. And even in saying we mustn't assume we all understand it, we often forget to spell out what it is we mustn't assume! But since we see here that even an apostle such as Peter needed to learn more about what it means to be justified by faith, it's likely that we do too!

> If even Peter needed to learn more about justification by faith, it's likely that we do too!

So first, we should connect the concept of justification-by-faith with Paul's controversy with Peter. Essentially, the dispute was about cleanliness. Jews did not eat with Gentiles because they were "unclean", and you had to be "clean" to worship God.

When Peter refrained from eating with Gentiles, Paul reminded him of what he had learned through revelation (Acts 11:8-10; 15:8-9), that in Christ we are "clean". In the Old Testament, you had to be "clean"—keeping the ceremonial laws—to go to worship, to be acceptable in the eyes and presence of God. Though the word "clean" does not show up in verses 11-13, that is what "circumcision" (**v 12**) and eating and all the rules and regulations were about.

It's in this context that Paul introduces "justification" (**v 15-16**). So "justification" is essentially the same thing as being "clean". To be justified is to be acceptable for fellowship with God.

Why does Paul switch terms? The word "justification" has a legal reference, and therefore it provides a different perspective on our salvation in Christ. The opposite of "clean" is "polluted"; but "cleansing" isn't sufficient to convey what Christ does for us. Cleanliness alone suggests that God accepts us because Christ "cleanses" and gets rid of our sinful thoughts and habits; so we become acceptable to God by actually becoming righteous in our attitudes and actions.

But the opposite of "justified" is "condemned". Justification means that in Christ, though we are actually sinners, we are not under condemnation. God accepts us despite our sin. We are not acceptable to God because we actually become righteous: we become actually righteous because we are acceptable to God.

J.I. Packer helpfully summarizes what Paul means:

"To 'justify' in the Bible means … to declare … of a man on trial, that he is not liable to any penalty, but is entitled to all the privileges due to those who have kept the law. Justifying is the act of a judge pronouncing the opposite sentence to condemnation—that of acquittal and legal immunity."

(*God's Words*, pages 139-140)

Not by Observing the Law

If we are justified by faith in what Christ has done, we are also *not* justified by what we do. Law-observance is not what saves (**v 16**).

That's what Paul means when he says: "Through the law I died to the law" (**v 19**). He can't mean that we no longer obey the law of God at all. Consider all the rest of Paul's writings. Doesn't he tell Christians that they must obey the law? For example, Paul tells the Corinthians that sexual immorality is wrong, and he bases this on what Genesis says about marriage (1 Corinthians 6:15-16).

What it does mean is that Paul died to the law *as a way of being saved*. He died to the law's condemnation. If we are not justified by the law, but by Christ (**Galatians 2:16**), then the law cannot condemn us. If I am feeling condemned and if I fear that God will no longer hear my prayers or care for me, then I have simply forgotten that I am dead to the law. I've forgotten that it can't harm me.

How did Paul die to seeking salvation-by-law-keeping "through the law"? Because it was as he tried to obey it that he realized that he simply couldn't. Paul is saying: *I would not have known what sin was except through the law. And I would not have known how unable I am to keep the law except through the law.* It was by really listening to the law that Paul saw he needed a Savior.

Living for God

If verses 16 and 19 become clear when we look closely at them, the same cannot really be said for verses 17-18, which are quite obscure! Perhaps the best way to read them is as saying: *If someone who knows they are justified by faith sins, is it because justification-by-faith-in-Christ promotes sin? Not at all! But if someone who professes faith in Christ keeps on with the same sinful lifestyle, rebuilding the sinfulness that Christ died to destroy the penalty for, making no effort to change, then it proves that this person never really grasped the gospel, but was just looking for an excuse to live in disobedience to God.* So it's likely that Paul is thinking of two different people in these two verses: a justified and repentant sinner in the first, and a non-justified and unrepentant rebel in the second.

Verse 19 is Paul's brief commentary on how someone who is truly justified by faith will view life. Because Paul died to the law, he can now "live for God". The implication is that before he came to faith, while he was trying to save himself through keeping the law, *Paul never really lived for God.* He was being very moral and good—but it was all for Paul, never for God.

> Paul was being very moral and good—but it was all for Paul, never for God.

When Paul was obeying God without knowing he was accepted, he was obeying to get a reward—for what he could get from God, not out of sheer love for God Himself. Now that he is justified and accepted, Paul has a new motive for obedience that is far more wholesome and powerful. He wants simply to live for the one "who loved me and gave himself for me" (**v 20**).

We will see much more about this in Galatians 5. For now, Paul wants us to understand that our acceptance gives us a new and stronger motive for obeying God than justification by works ever could.

Here, then, is a paraphrase of **verse 19**: *The law itself showed me that I could never make myself acceptable through it. So I stopped "living to it". I died to it as my savior. Though I obeyed God before, it was simply to get something from Him; it was for my own sake. Now I obey Him simply to please Him. I now live for Him.*

> Our acceptance gives us a new and stronger motive for obeying God.

This helps us to make sense of, and understand the life-changing implications of, **verse 20**. There's an apparent tension in these two sentences: Paul says "I no longer live" and then he says "the life I live". But in fact, this tension describes the way we should see our lives as Christians.

Verse 20 on its own would suggest we just sit back and let Christ give us the power to live rightly. Verse 21 alone would mean we have to do it all ourselves. The two sentences (which are one sentence in Greek) taken *together* show us that we are to live out our life on the basis of who we are in Christ.

Verse 20 is a restatement of verse 14: we need to live our lives "in line" with the truth of the gospel. Now that Christ's life is my life, Christ's past is my past. I am "in Christ" (**v 17**), which means that I am as free from condemnation before God as if I had already died and been judged, as if I had paid the debt myself. And I am as loved by God as if I had lived the life Christ lived. So "it is not me that lives, but Christ" is a triumphant reminder that, though "we ourselves are sinners", in Christ we are righteous.

Then Paul follows up with **verse 21**, to say: *Now when I live my life and make my choices and do my work, I do so remembering who I am by faith in Christ, who loved me so much!* The inner dynamic for living the Christian life is right here! Only when I see myself as completely loved and holy in Christ will I have the power to repent with joy, conquer my fears, and obey the One who did all this for me.

Everything or Nothing?

It's worth remembering that Paul is still speaking to Peter here! And so he finishes by reminding Peter that the Christian life is about living in line with the gospel throughout the whole of life, for the whole of our lives. We must go on as Christians as we started as Christians. After all, if at any point and in any way "righteousness could be gained through the law, Christ died for nothing!" (**v 21**). Christ will do everything for you, or nothing. You cannot combine merit and grace. If justification is by the law in any way, Christ's death is meaningless in history and meaningless to you personally.

> Christ will do everything for you, or nothing.

Imagine that your house were burning down but your whole family had escaped, and I said to you: *Let me show you how much I love you!* and ran into the house and died. *What a tragic and pointless waste of a life*, you would probably think. But now imagine that your house was on fire and one of your children was still in there, and I said to you: *Let me show you how much I love you!*, ran into the flames, and saved your child but perished myself. You would think: *Look at how much that man loved us.*

If we could save ourselves, Christ's death is pointless, and means nothing. If we realize we cannot save ourselves, Christ's death will mean everything to us. And we will spend the life that He has given us in joyful service of Him, bringing our whole lives into line with the gospel.

Questions for reflection

1. Is Christ's death everything to you? What difference does this make to your love for Him and your actions in life?

2. How would you explain "justification by faith" to someone who has never been to church before?

3. How would you explain the difference between being moral and being a Christian to someone who thinks being good makes them acceptable to God?

5. YOU NEVER LEAVE IT BEHIND

The first five verses of chapter 3 make a remarkable claim—one which is much missed *by* Christians, yet is absolutely critical *for* Christians.

Paul has shown in the second half of chapter 2 that we are saved when we stop trusting in our moral efforts or the law (we die to it) and trust in the work of Christ, which creates a whole new motivation for everything we do (we live to God). The gospel is the way we enter the kingdom of God. But now, Paul will show that the gospel is much *more* than that. We are not only *saved* by the gospel, but we also now *grow* by the gospel. Paul is saying that we don't begin by faith and then proceed and grow through our works. We are not only justified by faith in Christ, we are also **sanctified** by faith in Christ. We never leave the gospel behind.

That's what Paul is stating in 3:1-5, but really it's the subject of the whole of chapters 3 and 4. In 3:6-14 he will make a case for this from the Scriptures. 3:15-25 uses the example of a legal will to underline it, and to discuss the role of the law of God in a gospel-based life. 3:26 – 4:20 picks up on the example of adoption, and discusses the privileges of being brought into God's family. And 4:21-31 returns to Scripture to look at the life of **Abraham** and his two sons, pulling together the threads of the two chapters.

Christ Clearly Portrayed

In verses 1-3, Paul reminds the Galatian Christians how it was that they came to Christ from **paganism**. And in essence, "Jesus Christ was clearly portrayed as crucified" (**v 1**). This portrayal was achieved through preaching, through "what you heard" (**v 2, 5**). Paul isn't referring to a literal picture, but a **metaphorical** one.

There was a message communicated—"Jesus Christ … crucified" (see 1 Corinthians 2:1-5). Notice that the essence of this message is not how to live, but what Jesus has done for us on the cross. The gospel is an announcement of historical events before it is instructions on how to live. It is the proclamation of what has been done for us before it is a direction of what we must do.

But it also says that this message gripped the heart. Jesus was "clearly portrayed". The NIV translates the Greek as "clearly"; it also means "graphically", "vividly". This probably is a reference to the preaching's power. It was not dry and lecture-like. It "painted a picture" of Jesus, giving the hearers a moving view of what Christ did. "Our gospel came to you not simply with words, but also with power, with the Holy Spirit and with deep conviction" (1 Thessalonians 1:4). A Christian is not someone who knows about Jesus, but one who has "seen" Him on the cross. Our hearts are moved when we see not just that He died, but that He died *for us*. We see the meaning of His work for us. We are saved by a rationally clear *and* heart-moving presentation of Christ's work on our behalf.

> Our hearts are moved when we see not just that Jesus died, but that He died *for us*.

This is what had happened to these Galatians. "They believ[ed] what [they] heard" (**v 2b**). **Verses 2 and 3** are parallel sentences; Paul is underlining a point through repetition. He contrasts "believing" with "observing the law", and "beginning with the Spirit" with "attain[ing] … by human effort". To "believe" the gospel is not merely to assent to assertions about Christ (eg: He died, He rose) but to stop trying to attain salvation by observing the law. The word Paul uses for "attaining your goal" in **verse 3** is *epi-teleo,* "completion". He is describing our normal course of life. We are all striving to "complete" ourselves—to make ourselves acceptable to God, ourselves, and others—and we trust our efforts to attain that through moral, vocational, and relational achievements. Paul says that believing the gospel ("what you heard") means abandoning that entire approach. We stop "observing the law" (**v 2**) or "trying to attain [our] goal" (**v 3**).

Before we became Christians, we trusted various projects of personal effort to make us feel complete. But to "believe" in Christ is to enact a revolution in what we trust for our sense of *epi-teleo,* our completion or perfection.

An old hymn written by James Proctor sums it up well:
Lay your deadly "doing" down—
Down at Jesus' feet.
Stand in Him, in Him alone—
Gloriously complete.

The result of believing the vividly-portrayed gospel of Christ was that the Galatians "received the Spirit" (**v 2**). The Holy Spirit enters a life through belief in salvation by grace alone through Christ alone. The new birth Paul is describing is directly and inextricably connected to believing the gospel. This is why Jesus can say that we are given new birth through the Spirit (John 3:5), yet James (James 1:18) and Peter (1 Peter 1:23) can say we are given new birth through the word of God. They are indivisibly linked. The Spirit does not work apart from the gospel. The gospel is the channel and form of the Spirit's power.

Human Effort

But in these Christians' lives, something has changed. They had believed what they heard about Christ crucified; they had received the Spirit; but now they are "foolish" and "bewitched" (**v 1**).

Paul is not holding back here! What has gone wrong? In **verse 3**, Paul comes to his major "beef" with the Galatian Christians and the false teachers. He says that the way the Spirit entered your life should be the very same way the Spirit advances in your life. He says this twice, strongly: "After beginning with the Spirit, are you now trying to attain your goal by human effort?" (**v 3**). The Greek word translated "effort" is *sarki*, "flesh": "Are you trying to attain your goal through the flesh?" Since this term is parallel to "observing the law" in **verse 2**, the NIV translators conclude that to be "in the flesh" means to fail to remember or believe the gospel, and to seek completion through self-trusting "effort". As Dick Kaufmann, who used to be executive pastor at the church I serve, says:

> The way the Spirit entered your life is the way the Spirit advances in your life.

"Christians think that we are saved by the gospel, but then we grow by applying biblical principles to every area of life. But we are not just saved by the gospel, we grow by applying the gospel to every area of life."

In **verse 5**, Paul is even stronger. He moves into the present tense and says that right now the works of the Spirit—even miracles—occur "because you believe" (not "because you believed") and because you no longer "observe the law". The Spirit works as Christians don't rely on their own works, but rather consciously and continuously rest in Christ alone for their acceptability and completeness. Paul links the Spirit and the gospel in the most inseparable terms. The Spirit works as you apply and use the gospel.

Gospel Re-Depiction

We will see as we progress through Galatians that our failure to obey and conform to Christ's character is not a matter of simple lack of will-power, and so we cannot treat our failures simply by "trying harder". After all, resolving to "try harder" is resolving to rely on our own efforts to keep a law. We need instead to realize that the root of all our disobedience is particular ways in which we continue to seek control of our lives through systems of works-righteousness.

The way to progress as a Christian is continually to repent and up-root these systems in the same way that we became Christians—by the vivid depiction (and re-depiction) of Christ's saving work for us, and the abandoning of self-trusting efforts to complete ourselves. We must go back again and again to the gospel of Christ crucified, so that our hearts are more deeply gripped by the reality of what He did and who we are in Him.

So, we should not simply say: *Lord, I have a problem with anger. Please remove it by your power! Give me the power to forgive.* Rather, we should apply the gospel to ourselves at that point. Paul would tell us that uncontrolled bitterness is a result of not living in line with the gospel. It means that though we began with Jesus as Savior, some-thing has now become our **functional** savior in place of Jesus. Instead of believing that Christ is our hope and goodness, we are looking to something else as a hope, to some other way to make us feel good and complete.

Instead of just hoping God will remove our anger or simply exercis-ing will-power against it, we should ask: *If I am being angry and unfor-giving, what is it that I think I need so much? What is being withheld that I think that I must have if I am to feel complete, to have hope, to be a person of worth?* Usually, deep anger is because of something like that. It might be that we want comfort above all other things, and someone has made our lives harder, so we grow angry with them. It might be that we're worship-ing other people's approval and so get angry with anyone who in some way thwarts our bid for popularity and respect.

Comfort, approval, and con-trol; these are functional saviors. When they are blocked, we get

> Comfort, approval, control; these are functional saviors. When they are blocked, we get bitter.

bitter. The answer is not simply trying harder to directly control anger. It is repenting for the self-righteousness and the lack of rejoicing in the finished work of Christ which is at the root of the anger. As we make our hearts "look" at Christ crucified, the Spirit will work in us to replace that functional savior with *the* Savior; and the root of our anger will wither.

Questions for reflection

1. Are you in danger of forgetting that the gospel is the source of your ongoing acceptance? How, and why?

2. How do you "re-depict" Christ to yourself? Could you do this more?

3. Think of a sin that you regularly commit. What are you worshipping more than Jesus that causes you to decide to disobey Him? How will you replace that false savior with your true Savior next time you're tempted?

PART TWO

Meet Abraham

Paul now wants us to "consider Abraham" (**v 6**). It seems a strange link from verse 5; but in fact it is a masterstroke. Remember, Paul is countering the claims of the Judaizing teachers, who say: *It's great that you have faith in Christ; now, to remain acceptable to God, you need to live as Jews.* And the father of the Jews is Abraham. The people of Israel began when God promised Israel's ancestor, Abraham, that He would make his descendants into a great nation, living in a God-given land, blessed by God (Genesis 12:1-3).

But here, Paul is calling Abraham as a witness for his case. *Consider Abraham*, he says to these Gentile Christians, *because the ancestor of the Jews will show you that you really have been "bewitched" (v 1) by these Judaizing teachers.* Why? Because when we look at Abraham, we see a man who "believed God, and it was credited to him as righteousness" (**v 6**). What is most important about Abraham is that he was a "man of faith" (**v 9**). Paul is saying: *The father-founder of the Jewish people would agree with me.*

> What is most important about Abraham is that he was a "man of faith".

In **verse 6**, Paul is quoting from Genesis 15:6 (where Abraham is still known as "Abram"). The Greek word Paul uses is *elogisthan,* from the word *logos,* to speak. It means to be "declared" or "accounted". It was usually an accounting term that meant that money was being received and counted as payment toward some end. In general, the English term "credited" means the same thing—to confer a status on something that was not there before. If you "lease to buy" a house, it means that your rent payments can be used to purchase the house if you later so choose. At the moment that decision is made, your rent payments are credited to you as mortgage payments. A new status is conferred on them.

So what does it mean that Abraham's faith was "credited to him as righteousness"? Of course faith in God's word and promise *results in* righteousness! If we believe God exists, and that we owe Him our obedience and worship, then out of that will flow righteous living.

But here we have something more; something unique, and counter-intuitive. This is faith *counted as* righteousness. When the Bible tells us God credits Abraham's faith as righteousness, it means that God is treating Abraham as if he were living a righteous life.

> Here we have something unique: faith *counted* as righteousness.

Many commentators have resisted the remarkable implications of Genesis 15:6, and argued that we are being told that Abram's faith is itself a *form of* righteousness that pleases God; that his faith was an act of obedience that merited God's favor, a kind of righteousness. But the text doesn't say that his faith *was* righteousness; rather it was counted *as* (ie: as if it were) righteousness.

Douglas Moo writes:

> "If we compare other verses in which the same grammatical construction is used as in Genesis 15:6 we arrive at the conclusion ... that the [crediting] of Abram's faith as righteousness means 'to account him a righteousness that does not inherently belong to him'." (*The Epistle to the Romans*, page 262)

When God "credits righteousness", He is conferring a legal status on someone. He treats them as actually righteous and free from condemnation, even though they are still actually unrighteous in their heart and behavior. They are "justified".

This flies in the face of all traditional religion, which tells us that *either* we are living righteously and are therefore pleasing and acceptable to God, *or* we are living unrighteously and are therefore alienated from God. But Paul (and Abraham) are showing that it is possible to be loved and accepted by God while we are ourselves sinful and imperfect. Martin Luther's famous phrase is that Christians are *simul justus et peccator*— simultaneously righteous and sinful.

> It is possible to be loved and accepted by God while we are sinful and imperfect.

Paul makes the same point in Romans when he says that God "justifies the wicked" (Romans 4:5—notice that in this chapter, just as in Galatians 3, Paul cites Abraham as supporting his argument). When a person receives credited righteousness (ie: is justified), he or she is still wicked! The justified status is not given to them because they have gotten their hearts into a certain level of submission and worship. You don't clean up your life in order to earn credited righteousness. Rather, you receive it even while you are a sinner.

Be like Abraham

This is why Paul says: "Those who believe are children of Abraham" (**v 7**). What matters is not physical descent from Abraham (being Jewish), but spiritual descent (having the same faith as he did). "Those who *have faith* are blessed along with Abraham" (**v 9**).

So, what does it mean to "have faith" like Abraham? First, he shows us that saving faith is believing the gospel-promise. "He believed God, and it was credited to him as righteousness" (**v 6**). Notice that it does not say that Abraham believed *in* God (though he certainly did!). Believing in God is not saving faith (James 2:19 says that even "the demons believe"). Rather, he had to believe and trust what God actually said in His promise to save.

You can't believe God without believing in God, but you can believe in God without believing God! Saving faith is different from generic general faith in the existence of God, or even in the doctrines and teachings of the Bible in general.

Second, Abraham shows that saving faith is faith in God's provision, not our performance. Abraham was childless (Genesis 15:2), with a **barren** wife. He could not have children—yet God promised that his offspring would be as innumerable as the stars (v 5-6). God would come down into history and do a mighty deed that did not depend on human ability at all. The promise of an heir depended wholly on God, not on Abraham at all. Abraham had to believe that God would do it. And in Genesis 15, Abraham did.

Two Types of People

Abraham was a "man of faith" (**Galatians 3:9**). But there is another way to live. We can "rely on observing the law" (**v 10**). This person "live[s] by them [the law]" (**v 12**). To "live by" something means to rely on it for our happiness and fulfillment. Whatever we live by is essentially the bottom line of our lives—what gives us meaning, confidence, and definition. It is very illuminating to ask: *What do I live by? What is my life based on? What, if I lost it, would make me feel as if I had no life left?* These are all questions that lay bare the foundation of your life.

To have Abraham-like faith brings blessing (**v 9**). The result of living by the law is that we are "under a curse" (**v 10**). This "curse" has two aspects. Theologically, anyone who says: *I can be saved by obeying the law* must then be prepared to really look at what the law commands. To love God wholly, we would have to obey the law wholly. To be blessed by God instead of cursed by Him, we would have to look at the law and satisfy its every demand. And that cannot be done. Objectively, attempting salvation-by-law-observance means we are cursed.

This means that, psychologically, everyone who is seeking to save themselves by their own performance will experience a curse subjectively. At the very least, attempting to be saved by works will lead to profound anxiety and insecurity, because you can never be sure that you are living up to your standards sufficiently, whatever they may be. This makes you over-sensitive to criticism, envious and intimidated by others who outshine you. It makes you nervous and timid (because you are unsure of where you stand) or else swaggering and boastful (because you are trying to convince yourself of where you stand). Either way, you live with a sense of curse and condemnation.

> Attempting to be saved by works makes you over-sensitive, envious and intimidated.

The Curse Removed

How, then, can we escape the curse and enjoy the blessing promised to the nations (**v 8**)? Of course, it is all because of what Jesus did.

He brought us into blessing by "becoming a curse for us" (**v 13**). Paul quotes Deuteronomy 21:23: "Cursed is everyone who is hung on a tree". When a person was executed in the Old Testament, it was usually by stoning. Then the body was hung on a tree as a symbol of divine rejection. It was not that the man was cursed because he was hung, but rather, he was hung as a sign of his curse. Paul draws the connection to Christ, whose execution was on a cross-tree to show that He experienced the curse of divine rejection. There, He freed us ("redeemed us") from the curse of the law by taking it for us.

The word "for" means "on behalf of" or "in the place of"; Jesus was our substitute. He received the curse we earned (**v 13**) so that we might receive the blessing He earned (**v 14**). Our sins and curse are given, or imputed, to Him: His righteousness and blessing and Spirit are imputed to us. It is a two-fold imputation.

Notice that Paul doesn't simply say that Jesus redeemed us by "taking a curse" but by "becoming a curse". This is parallel to 2 Corinthians 5:21: "God made him who had no sin to be sin for us, so that in him we might become the righteousness of God". Jesus was treated as if He were a sinner; He was treated as liable for all that a wicked person would be liable for. Legally speaking, He *became* sin.

Why is that so important to realize? Because it shows the stunning claim regarding what happens to us when we believe. If Jesus "became" a sinner for us, then we have "become" righteous in the same way. If His taking the curse means that He was regarded by God as a sinner, then our receiving the blessing means that we are regarded by God as if we are perfectly righteous and flawless.

Salvation means much more than forgiveness. We do not simply have our slate wiped clean; we also become perfect in God's sight. And we stay perfect in God's sight. We do not begin by trusting in Christ's curse-becoming, blessing-giving death for us, and then continue "by human effort", as though we must now earn ongoing blessing. That is "foolish" (**v 1**). We go on as we began, having our hearts melted and molded by knowing and trusting Christ crucified. We never move on from the gospel—we never can, and never need to.

Questions for reflection

1. How does having righteousness credited to us change the way we see ourselves? Our Christian lives? Jesus Christ?

2. Have you experienced, or witnessed others experiencing, the psychological "curse" of living by the law?

3. Which truth in Galatians 3:13-14 excites you most today?

6. THE LAW IN THE GOSPEL LIFE

Whenever we hear the radical claims of salvation-by-grace, we should immediately be prompted to ask: *If we are "free from the law", does that mean we don't have to obey the law of God? If I am always saved only by Christ's performance and not my own, why should I strive to live a holy life? Do I have any obligation to keep God's law, and why?*

In fact, there is no more practical question than that of the relationship of a Christian to the law of God. Our other questions about how to live—*How should I treat my spouse? What shall I spend my money on? What corners can I cut in my job?*—stem from the central question: *What is my relationship as a Christian to God's law?*

In the flow of his letter to the Galatians, Paul has established that we are saved, justified, redeemed only by faith in Christ, and not through any righteousness of our own. So he has reached the point where a careful reader will be asking the question about how the law fits. And so he addresses this crucial issue here.

Making a Will

First, though, Paul wants to underline what the law does *not* do. So he takes "an example from everyday life" (**v 15**). He points out that human contracts are binding and difficult or impossible to void. "As no one can set aside or add to a human covenant that has been duly established, so it is in this case" (**v 15**). The word Paul uses is *diatheke* (translated "covenant" in the NIV), a word for a legal will.

This, of course, is a good example, since once a will is duly and legally made, we consider it binding no matter what changes in conditions may occur. So it is with God's promises. For example, if a woman leaves her poor daughter more money than her rich daughter, that legal document will be binding even if the rich daughter loses all her wealth the day after her mother dies. The will holds despite new conditions.

Paul knows that some might see that Moses' law was "introduced 430 years later" than God's promises of salvation to Abraham (**v 17**), and conclude: *Ah! This changes things! If we are to get the blessing of Abraham, we will now have to obey the law of Moses.*

But Paul says, and shows, that this is a false conclusion: "The law … does not set aside the covenant previously established by God and thus do away with the promise" (**v 17**). The law of Moses cannot turn God's promise to Abraham into something other than what it is—a promise. How can the coming of the law change the very nature of God's promise to Abraham that there would be a supernatural intervention, by grace, to provide blessing (Genesis 12:1-2; 15:1-6)?

This is a powerful argument. If the law of Moses came as a way of salvation, then it means that God had changed His mind. It would mean that God had decided that we didn't need a Savior, and that He would give out His blessing on the basis of performance, not promise.

> If the law was a way of salvation, it would mean that God had decided we didn't need a Savior.

If the law had this function, it would not add to the promise; it would "do away" with it altogether (**v 17**). "For if the inheritance depends on the law, then it no longer depends on a promise" (**v 18**). The principle is that the very concepts of "promise" and "law" are mutually exclusive. If I give you something because of what I have promised, it is not because of your performance. If I give you something because of what you have done, it is not because of my promise. Paul is adamant: either something comes by grace or works; either it comes because of the giver's promise or the receiver's performance. It is either one or the other.

This is worth reflecting on. For a promise to bring a result, it needs only to be believed, but for a law to bring a result, it has to be obeyed. For example, if I say to you: *My Uncle Jack wants to meet you and give you $10 million dollars*, the only way you can probably fail to receive the $10 million is to fail to believe the claim. If you just laugh and go home, rather than going to see Uncle Jack, you may never get the money. But if, on the other hand, I say to you: *My Uncle Jack is willing to leave you his inheritance of $10 million dollars, but you have to go live with him and take care of him in his old age*, then you have to fulfill the requirement and condition if you are to get the money.

A gift-promise needs only to be believed to be received, but a law-wage must be obeyed to be received.

Covenant Promise

If the law of Moses was intended to be the means for salvation, then the promise to Abraham would not have been a real promise. And "in this case", the promise is sealed by a covenant. Paul is taking us back once more to Genesis 15. When Abram asks God: "How can I know that I will gain possession" of the promised blessing (v 8), God tells him to get a cow, a goat, a ram, a dove and a pigeon. Abram knows what to do with them—he "cut them in two and arranged the halves opposite each other" (v 10). This seems strange to us, but in Abram's day this was the way a covenant was "signed". Each covenant-maker would pass between the halves of the animals. It was a (very!) graphic way of those entering a covenant saying: *If I break this agreement, may I be cut up and cut off: I will deserve to die just like these animals did.*

What's astonishing in the covenant between God and Abram is that Abram never walks between the halves! "Abram fell into a deep sleep" (v 12). The only thing that passes through is "a smoking fire-pot with a blazing torch [which] appeared and passed between the pieces" (v 17). What is this strange fire? It's God—"on that day the Lord made a covenant with Abram" (v 18).

The promise by God to Abram is a covenantal promise. And it is a covenant that relies in no way on Abram, but only on God. He would die before He broke His promise to bless Abram and His descendants, and through one particular descendant ("your seed", **Galatians 3:16**) to offer blessing to the world. And in the end, He did die, on a cross, as that "seed", the man Jesus Christ.

> The covenant relies in no way on Abram, but only on God.

With Genesis 15 in mind, Paul is simply pointing out to the Galatians the impossibility of God adding obedience-demands to His covenantal promise. He had Himself guaranteed that He would keep His promise—how and why then could the law "do away with the promise" (**v 17**)?

Therefore, the law of Moses must have a different purpose.

But before we move on to see what God's purpose in giving the law was, we need to ask what direct relevance Paul's argument here would have had to the Galatian Christians (and to us today). They were not part of physical Israel, and were not alive either when the promises were given to Abraham, or when the law was given to Moses.

And yet, in their own lives, they were in danger of the same misunderstanding as Paul here argues against in redemptive history. The misreading that Paul is correcting is that God promised to bless His people, but that this blessing was achieved or kept by law-obedience. And, as Paul has already pointed out, the Galatian Christians were, "after beginning with the Spirit ... now trying to attain [their] goal by human effort" (v 3). Paul is establishing that an offer which begins by grace, as a free promise, must continue to be made on the same basis—or stop being a promise. As soon as it becomes based on performance, it can no longer be a free gift. This was no less true of the Galatians' acceptability before God than it was of ancient Israel's.

It is common for believers to begin their Christian lives by looking beyond themselves at "Christ ... clearly ... crucified" (v 1), relying on God's promise that Christ has taken our curse and given us His blessing. But, as we go on, it is tempting, and easy, to look within ourselves at our own "human effort" (v 3), resting in our own performance to give us our sense of acceptability before God. Doing this makes us radically insecure—it cuts away our assurance, and prompts us to despair or pride.

Paul wants the Galatian Christians to turn their ears from the false teachers so that they will drag their eyes away from themselves and back to the cross. Whatever the reason that God commands His people how to live, it cannot be in order to gain acceptance from Him. The promise precedes the law. The law cannot co-exist with the promise in bringing blessing; the law does not set aside the promise as the source of blessing. Israel was a nation which was to rely on God's promise; the individual Christian no less so.

Questions for reflection

1. How do the details of God's covenant-making ceremony with Abram encourage you?

2. When are you most tempted to look to your own efforts to make yourself acceptable to God?

3. To help you diagnose your own heart, ask yourself: What causes me to feel despair in life? What makes me feel proud about myself?

PART TWO

The Purpose of the Law

At last, in **verse 19**, Paul tells us what the point of the law is! It was "added because of **transgressions**" (**v 19**) until Christ came. The law did not come to tell us about salvation, but about sin. Its main purpose is to show us our problem, that we are law-breakers; and to prove to us that we cannot be the solution, since we are unable to be perfect law-keepers.

The rest of **verse 19** and **verse 20** is extremely cryptic. Some commentators think Paul is saying that God spoke the law to the people through a **mediator**, namely **Moses**, but that He spoke the promise directly to Abraham. But this is not at all certain. No one is sure what Paul means or how this fits into the argument. Fortunately, the thrust of Paul's argument and its other supporting points are clear, so it is not urgent that we decode these sentences to understand him.

In **verse 21**, Paul returns to the statement with which he began **verse 19**. God never intended His law to "**impart** life", otherwise we could become righteous through it. In fact, "the Scripture [ie: the Old Testament] declares that the whole world is a prisoner of sin" (**v 22**). Paul's Greek is a bit more vivid than the English here. He says, literally, that "Scripture imprisoned all the world to sin".

This is not a function of Scripture we tend to focus on! Paul is probably remembering his own experience just prior to conversion (see Romans 7:7-13). He had been a self-satisfied Pharisee until the law against coveting and envy really hit home (Romans 7:9 says "the commandment came [home]"). The law made him see (and feel) that he was morally helpless. He realized that he was not simply a sinner, but a prisoner of sin, helpless to free or cure himself.

> Paul realized that he was a prisoner of sin, helpless to free or cure himself.

This is the purpose of the law. It shows us that we do not just "fall short" of God's will, requiring some extra effort to do better, but that we are completely under sin's power, requiring a rescue.

The law has the power to show us that we are not righteous; but it cannot give us the power to be righteous. In fact, as we see God's standards and try and fail to keep them, the law shows us that we do not have that power. "Righteousness" cannot "come by the law" (**v 21b**). Ironically, if we think we can be righteous by the law, we have missed the main point of the law.

In summary, Paul says, the law shows us our sin "so that what was promised … might be given to those who believe" (**v 22b**). The law does its work to lead us toward recognition of our need for salvation-by-grace. The law, then, does not oppose the promise of salvation-by-grace-through-Christ but rather supports it, by pointing out to us our need of it.

Pointing to the Promise

Paul uses two metaphors to characterize the way the law works in a Christian's life.

First, the law is a guard. "Before this faith came, we were held prisoners by the law, locked up until faith should be revealed" (**v 23**). The Greek words for "held prisoners" and "locked up" mean to be protected by military guards.

Second, the law is a tutor, a *paidagogos,* under whose "supervision" (ie: tuition) we live. "The law was put in charge to lead us to Christ" (**v 24**). In the homes of Paul's day, the tutor or guardian was usually a slave who supervised the children on the parents' behalf. We will see this metaphor again in chapter 4.

In both cases, the guard and the tutor remove freedom. In both cases, the relationship with the "law" is not intimate or personal; it is based on rewards and punishments. And in both cases, we are treated as children or worse.

So Paul describes all non-gospel-based religion as being character-ized by:

(a) a sense of bondage

(b) an impersonal relationship with the divine, motivated by a desire for rewards and a fear of punishments

(c) anxiety about one's standing with God

But the second metaphor (unlike the first) shows us that the law's true purpose is instructive. It points beyond itself, just as the tutor seeks to prepare the children for lives as adults, as free persons. The law points to:

(a) a life not of confinement, but of freedom

(b) not an impersonal, but a personal relationship with God

(c) not immaturity, but maturity of character

And so the Old Testament demands that people "love the LORD your God with all your heart" (Deuterono-my 6:5) and that we must be "peo-ple who have my law in your hearts" (Isaiah 51:7). The law (if we are really listening to it) continually emphasizes that we need a righteousness, a pow-er, a love for God that is beyond our-selves and beyond the law. We need salvation-by-grace.

> We need a righteousness, a power, a love that is beyond ourselves.

John Stott is worth quoting at some length here:

"After God gave the promise to Abraham, He gave the law to Moses. Why? He had to make things worse before He could make them better. The law exposed sin, provoked sin, con-demned sin. The purpose of the law was to lift the lid off man's respectability and disclose what he is really underneath—sinful, rebellious, guilty, under the judgment of God and helpless to save himself.

And the law must still be allowed to do its God-given duty

today. One of the great faults of the contemporary church is
the tendency to soft-pedal sin and judgment ... We must never
bypass the law and come straight to the gospel. To do so is to
contradict the plan of God in biblical history ... No man has
ever appreciated the gospel until the law has first revealed him
to himself. It is only against the inky blackness of the night sky
that the stars begin to appear, and it is only against the dark
background of sin and judgment that the gospel shines forth."

(*The Message of Galatians*, pages 92-93)

Many Christians (though not all) testify that when they first became
aware of their need for God, they went through a time of immaturity
in which they became extremely religious. They diligently sought to
mend their ways and do religious duties to "clean up their lives". They
made tearful "surrenders" to God at church services. They "gave their
lives to Jesus" and "asked Him into their hearts". But so often, they
were really only resolving to be very good and very religious, hoping
that this would procure the favor and blessing of God. At this stage,
they tended to have a lot of emotional ups and downs (like children),
feeling good when they made a spiritual commitment and despond-
ent when they failed to keep a promise to God. They felt a great deal
of anxiety.

They were, as Paul says here, like children under a "tutor". They
were on their way to discovering God in the gospel, but they were
not there yet!

The Law in the Christian's Life

The law locked us up "until faith [was] revealed" (**v 24**). Once faith
had come, "we [were] no longer under the supervision [ie: tutelage]
of the law" (**v 25**).

Our efforts to gain God's approval by obedience to His law show us
that we must go beyond the law to find that approval. When we see
this, and allow Christ to be our Savior, we have learned the lesson the
law sought to teach us as our tutor.

But for the Christian, the law has already achieved its purpose of being our guard and our tutor. Does this mean we can now forget about it? Absolutely not (as Paul would say!).

As we saw above, the law was our "supervisor" until we found Christ, and was thus like a guardian over a child until he or she reaches maturity. But let's draw out the **analogy**. Is it the design of child-rearing that when the child grows to maturity he or she then casts off all the values of the parent or guardian and lives in a totally different way?

No. If all goes well, the adult child is no longer coerced into obedience as before, but now has internalized the basic values, and lives in a similar manner because he or she wants to.

So Paul is indicating not that we no longer have any relation to the values of God's law, but that we no longer view it as a system of salvation. It no longer forces obedience through coercion and fear. The gospel means that we no longer obey the law out of fear of rejection and hope of salvation-by-performance. But when we grasp salvation-by-promise, our hearts are filled with gratitude and a desire to please and be like our Savior—and the way to do that is through obeying the law. And once we come to the law motivated by gratitude, we are *better* in our obedience of the law than we ever were when we thought that our obedience might save us.

> We are filled with a desire to be like our Savior— and the way to do that is through obeying the law.

Why? First, if we think that law-obedience will save us, we become emotionally incapable of admitting just how searching and demanding it is. For example, Jesus says that to resent or disdain anyone is a form of murder (Matthew 5:21-22). Only if we know that we cannot keep it completely, but that we don't need to keep it at all to be saved because Christ did it for us, will we be able to admit just how broad and deep this command is. If we are seeking to be saved by our obedience of it, we will constantly be trying to limit the scope and application of God's law, in order to make it manageable for us to keep.

Second, grateful joy is a motive that will lead to much more endurance in obedience than fearful compliance. Fearful compliance makes obedience a drudgery that can't take adversity. In short, the gospel allows us truly to honor the law in a way that legalistic people cannot. Without the gospel, we may obey the law, but we will learn to hate it. We will use it, but we will not truly love it. Only if we obey the law because we are saved, rather than to be saved, will we do so "for God" (Galatians 2:19). Once we understand salvation-by-promise, we do not obey God any longer for our sake, by using the law-salvation-system to get things from God. Rather, we now obey God for His sake, using the law's content to please and delight our Father.

Law and grace work together in Christian salvation. Many people want a sense of joy and acceptance but they will not admit the seriousness of their sin. They will not listen to the law's searching and painful analysis of their lives and hearts. But unless we see how helpless and profoundly sinful we are, the message of salvation will not be exhilarating and liberating. Unless we know how big our debt is, we cannot have any idea of how great Christ's payment was. If we think that we are not all that bad, the idea of grace will never change us.

> If we think we are not all that bad, the idea of grace will never change us.

The law shows us as we really are. And so the law points us to see Christ as He really is: our Savior, the One who obeyed the law on our behalf and then died in our place so that we might receive the promised blessing. The law allows us to love Jesus, and enables us to show our love in grateful obedience to Him.

Questions for reflection

1. Think back to your conversion, or the first time you understood the gospel. How did your view of God's law change?

2. How does knowing God's law increase your gratitude to Christ? What difference does this make to your **affections**?

3. Why do *you* obey God's law? Do you ever obey it for the wrong reasons?

7. CHILDREN OF GOD

We've reached the climax of everything that Paul has said so far. In fact, we've reached the climax of the gospel:

"The notion that we are children of God, His own sons and daughters ... is the mainspring of Christian living ... Our sonship to God is the apex of creation and the goal of redemption"

(Sinclair Ferguson, *Children of the Living God*, pages 5-6).

If we want to understand who a Christian is, and why being a Christian is a privilege, we need to appreciate divine adoption. If Jesus, as "the Seed" (3:19), gets all of Abraham's promised blessings, then anyone who belongs to Christ through faith automatically becomes an heir of the promises to Abraham (**v 29**). How does this inheritance come to us? Through the Son, we become God's children legally (**4:4-5**), receiving a new status; and through the Spirit, we become God's children experientially (**v 6-7**).

> If we want to understand why being a Christian is a privilege, we need to appreciate divine adoption.

Sons of God

The heart of the Christian life is **3:26**: "You are all sons of God". We already *are* sons. It is not something we are aiming at; it is not a future attainment. It is something that we have already, in our present state.

But this sonship is not a universal given. We are not "children of God" in some general way, by virtue of having been created by Him. There is a sense in which all human beings are God's offspring because all humans have been made in His image (Acts 17:29). But Paul is speaking of a much deeper kind of relationship here. This sonship comes "through faith in Christ Jesus". We are only His sons when we have faith in *the* Son. It is through faith that God adopts us.

Many take offense at using the masculine word "sons" to refer to all Christians, male and female. Some would prefer to translate **verse 26**: "You are all children of God" (as the NIV 2011 does). But if we are too quick to correct the biblical language, we miss the revolutionary (and radically **egalitarian**) nature of what Paul is saying. In most ancient cultures, daughters could not inherit property. Therefore, "son" meant "legal heir", which was a status forbidden to women. But the gospel tells us we are *all* sons of God in Christ. We are *all* heirs. Similarly, the Bible describes all Christians together, including men, as the "bride of Christ" (Revelation 21:2). God is evenhanded in His gender-specific metaphors. Men are part of His Son's bride; and women are His sons, His heirs. If we don't let Paul call Christian women "sons of God", we miss how radical and wonderful a claim this is.

Clothed with Christ

How does faith in Christ mean we are treated as God's sons? **Verse 27**: through faith (the public sign of which is being "baptized into Christ"), Paul tells these believers they "have clothed yourselves with Christ". This clothing image is a favorite metaphor of Paul's (see Romans 13:12; Ephesians 4:24; Colossians 3:12). Here, he likens Christ Himself to a garment. And this idea of clothing ourselves with Christ implies four amazing things:

1. *Our primary identity is in Christ.* Our clothing tells people who we are. Nearly every kind of clothing is actually a uniform showing that we are identified with others of the same gender, social class or national group. But to say that Christ is our clothing is to say that our ultimate identity is found, not in any of these classifications, but in Christ.

2. *The closeness of our relationship to Christ.* Your clothes are kept closer to you than any other possession. You rely on them for shelter every moment. They go everywhere with you. So to say Christ is our clothing is to call us to moment-by-moment dependence and existential awareness of Christ. We are spiritually to "practice His presence".

3. *The imitation of Christ.* To practice the presence of Christ entails that we continually think and act as if we were directly before His face. A similar biblical phrase is to "walk before him" (see, for instance, Genesis 17:1; Psalm 56:13). It means to take Jesus into every area of life and change it in accordance with His will and Spirit. We are to "put on" His virtues and actions. We are to "dress up like Jesus".

4. *Our acceptability to God.* Finally, clothing is worn as adornment. It covers our nakedness; and God has been providing clothes which cover our shame since the fall (see Genesis 3:7, 21). To say that Christ is our clothing is to say that in God's sight, we are loved because of Jesus' work and salvation. When God looks at us, He sees us as His sons because He sees His Son. The Lord Jesus has given us His righteousness, His perfection, to wear.

> God has been providing clothes which cover our shame since the Fall.

So **Galatians 3:27** is a daring and comprehensive metaphor for a whole new life. It means to think of Christ constantly, to have His Spirit and His character infuse and permeate everything you think, say and do. This goes so far beyond the keeping of rules and regulations. This goes even beyond simple obedience. This is to be in love with Him, bathed in Him, awash in Him. A Christian can never need some additional commitment to the law of Moses in order to receive or maintain full acceptance with God. He or she is *clothed with Christ.*

One in Christ

Verse 26 reveals to us the amazing intimacy that exists between Christians and the Creator God, our Father. **Verse 27** outlines the wonderful closeness between Christians and God the Son, our Savior. **Verse 28** flows out of these two verses and shows us the unity between Christians. There is no division between different races, social strata, or genders.

This is *not* to say that there is no longer any *distinction* inside the church. It does not mean, for example, that Greeks should not keep their distinct Greek culture and consciousness—that they must become identical to Jews (that is one of the main points of the whole letter!). It cannot mean, therefore, that there should be no distinctions between male and female in the way we live. Paul's teaching in Ephesians 5:21 – 6:9 and Colossians 3:18 – 4:1 shows that he did not mean this statement to obliterate distinctive duties and practices for different cultures, classes, and genders. We are not all identical or interchangeable, but we are all "one."

> The gospel means I am Christian before I am anything else.

The gospel has radical social implications. It means I am a Christian before I am anyone or anything else. It means that all the barriers that separate people in the world into warring factions come down in Christ.

Paul picks up on the three barriers that usually divide people:

1. *The cultural barrier:* "neither Jew nor Greek". Cultural divisions are to have no part in the church of Christ. People of one culture do not need to become like another culture in order to be accepted by God. So we should accept one another without one group feeling or declaring the superiority of its cultural ways over another. Inside the church, we should associate with and love one another across racial and cultural barriers.

2. *The class barrier:* "neither ... slave nor free". Again, economic stratification should not extend into the church. People should not associate (as in the world) according to class but across such barriers. The poor or mod-estly paid worker must not be made to feel inferior in any way. On the other hand, the well-off must not be resented or shunned.

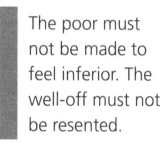

The poor must not be made to feel inferior. The well-off must not be resented.

3. *The gender barrier:* "neither ... male nor female". This was perhaps the strongest barrier of Paul's day. Women were considered abso-lutely inferior to men. Even today, the application of this principle is the most explosive and controversial. But, in any case, it was clearly revolutionary. Because women are equal in Christ before God, they must be seen to be equally gifted and able as men.

It is natural to ask: what was Paul's understanding of the implica-tions of **verse 28** for society in general? Was "neither ... slave nor free" a call for the abolition of slavery? If so, why does he tell slaves to be diligent in their work in Ephesians 6:5-8 and Colossians 3:22-25? Notice that his thesis in Galatians 3 is that this radical equality is for those who are in Christ. The implications of this for broader society were just that—implications, that have had to work themselves out over the years. For example, most of ancient society followed the law of "primogeniture": the oldest son inherited virtually the whole fam-ily estate. In this passage, Paul plays off of this custom to tell every Christian, male and female, that he or she is equally God's heir, heir to all of which Jesus is heir. Obviously, Paul is not forbidding the law of primogeniture in this text. That is not his direct concern. But just as obviously, Christian families who begin to think in this way, so subversive to pagan social attitudes, will have a tendency to drop the practice of primogeniture. In the long run, this truth of Paul's was bound to have an effect on how Christians lived in society at large.

The freedom of the gospel has to change our attitude toward everything in life. But broader social change is not Paul's immediate concern in this teaching. He wants the gospel to bring down barriers within the Christian community.

Only the truths of **verses 26-27** lead to this kind of unity. How? First, the good news of the gospel creates unity. The privileges we get in the gospel (sonship, v 26; the Spirit, v 14; perfect righteousness, v 10; all because of our union with Christ, v 27) are so stupendous that they have to surpass the greatest earthly merited or inherited advantages. How can I look down on someone who is clothed with Christ? Why would I ever be jealous of anyone else when I am a son of God?

Second, the bad news of the gospel creates unity. As recipients of grace, we know that our blessings come unearned, and so our pride in our race, status, or gender is removed. We know we are sinners like everyone else. There is no reason for us to think of ourselves as better than, or exclude, others. We are sinners, adopted by grace.

Heirs through Christ

Every verse of this section stretches our horizons, thrilling our hearts with all that we are through faith. **Verse 26** reaches upwards—we are sons of the Creator! **Verse 28** spans the globe—we are united with every other Christian, one in Christ regardless of anything that the world suggests should divide us.

Verse 29 looks back through history. By clothing ourselves with Christ through faith, "you are Abraham's seed, and heirs according to the promise". All that God promised Abraham, He has fulfilled and will fulfill in His Son, Jesus; and so all that God promised, we will enjoy as His adopted sons.

Questions for reflection

1. How do you feel about being an adopted son of God?

2. In which area of your life do you most struggle to remember that you're clothed with Christ? What difference would it make to practice the presence of Christ?

3. What barriers divide people in the area where you live? How are those broken down within your church; and what do you do to help this?

PART TWO

Coming of Age

The great truths of chapter 3:26-29 reach up, out and back. They will take a lifetime to appreciate, and they give us an eternity to enjoy them. So at the start of chapter 4, Paul pauses on these truths to help us continue to grasp what it means to be adopted by God.

> These truths take a lifetime to appreciate, and give us an eternity to enjoy them.

To illustrate our sonship, Paul uses the illustration of a young child who is the heir of a great estate. When he is a minor he is "no different from a slave" (**4:1**), since "he is subject to guardians and trustees" (**v 2**). But when he comes of age, he comes into his inheritance.

In ancient times, the process of "coming of age" was an important and well-defined process. A Roman child-heir was a minor under guardians until age 14, and was still to some degree under trustees until age 25. Not until then could the youth exercise complete, independent control over his estate.

What does it mean to be a "child ... no different from a slave" (**v 1**)? Paul's illustration applies to us spiritually on three different levels. Different commentators choose different levels, but I think they are all implied by the text.

First, it shows that, in the time of Moses' leadership, the people of God had spiritual liberty promised to them in their covenant with God made at **Mount Sinai**, but they had not yet come to possess and experience it. With a few exceptions, people under the Mosaic covenant did not experience the promised intimacy and freedom, because the means and assurance of forgiveness was general and vague (see Hebrews 10:1-4).

On a second level, this is a picture of all human beings. "So also when *we* were children, *we* were in slavery under the basic principles of the world" (**v 3**). Paul will outline more fully what he means by "basic principles" in verses 8-11 (see next chapter). But since most of the Galatians had not been born Jews, Paul must mean that all human beings are spiritual "slaves" before coming to Christ. We are all in a sense "under the law," even if we have never heard of the Bible or Moses. Why? Because we are all desperately trying to live up to some standards. We are anxious and burdened. Our relationship with the divine is remote or non-existent.

Finally, on a third level, this is a picture of how Christians may to some degree fail to experience the freedom and joy of their salvation. Christians can continue to live day by day as slaves, instead of as the adopted sons of God that they are. Paul will return to this in verses 8-9 (and 5:1). Though we are rich in the gospel, adopted children of God with complete and direct access to the Father, we can go back to relating to Him only through our record and moral merits. It's as though we are given a gift, but give it back to the giver so that we can strive to earn it.

Slavery is our natural state. But Paul is going to show first *how* people can "come of age"; and then how people can *enjoy being* of age.

The Work of the Son

"When the time had fully come" (**v 4**)—in history, and in our own ex-perience—"God sent his Son". It is the Son who makes us "of age".

How? First by "redeem[ing] those under the law" (**v 5**), removing all penalty or debt. In a sense we belong to the law—we are "under" its mastery, slaves to it. We are obligated to keep it, but we cannot.

So God sent His Son "born of a woman" (**v 4**)—a real human be-ing—and He sent Him "born under law". Jesus was born, as all hu-man beings are, into a state of obligation to God's law. But Jesus is uniquely able to "redeem those under the law." This is the same word that is used for "redeem" in 3:13. It means to release a slave from his or her owner by paying the slave's full price. Here, the slave master is the law. Jesus pays our full price to the law. He completely fulfills all the law's demands on us. And so He is able to free us from it.

Second, Jesus procures for us "the full rights of sons" (**v 5**). The RSV translation renders this "adoption as sons". Both the NIV and RSV are trying to convey the sense of a single word. Literally, through Christ we receive "the sonship". This is a legal term. In the Greco-Roman world, a childless, wealthy man could take one of his servants and adopt him. At the moment of adoption, he ceased to be a slave and received all the financial and legal privileges within the estate and outside in the world as the son and heir. Though by birth he was a slave without a relationship with the father, he now receives the legal status of son. It is a new life of privilege. It is a remarkable metaphor for what Jesus has given us.

So to understand what God sent His Son to do, we need to travel to an ancient slave market to appreciate redemption, and to an ancient wealthy household to grasp the concept of sonship. Only *together* do they give us a complete picture of what Christ has accomplished for us.

> To understand why God sent His Son, we need to travel to a slave market, and to a wealthy household.

Yet it is very easy and common to think of our salvation only in terms of the first and not the second—that is, only as the transfer *from us* of our sins, but not as the transfer *to us* of the Son's rights and privileges. When we think like that, we are really only "half-saved by grace". We can get pardon, but now we have to live a good life to earn and maintain God's favor and rewards. Paul wants to show the Galatians, and us, that not only did Christ remove the curse we deserved (3:13; **4:5a**), but He also gives us the blessing He deserved (3:14; **4:5b**). God's honor and reward are just as secure and guaranteed as our pardon.

To use another image, Jesus' salvation is not only like receiving a pardon and release from death row and prison. Then we'd be free, but on our own, left to make our own way in the world, thrown back on our own efforts if we're to make anything of ourselves.

But in the gospel, we discover that Jesus has taken us off death row and then has hung around our neck the Congressional Medal of Honor. We are received and welcomed as heroes, as if we had accomplished extraordinary deeds.

Unless we remember this, we will be anxious and even despairing when we sin or fail. We will think our slate has been wiped clean, but now it is up to us to write good deeds on that slate so that God will love us and accept us. That is where we are left if we remember only half of **verse 5**. But our slate has been wiped clean *and* Jesus has written His righteousness onto it. Our inheritance is not a prize to be won. It is a gift from Christ.

The Work of the Spirit

Verse 6—"God sent the Spirit"—parallels **verse 4**—"God sent his Son". The Son's purpose was to secure for us the *legal status* of our sonship. By contrast, the Spirit's purpose is to secure the *actual experience* of it.

This is not like the work of the Son. The work of the Son brings us an **objective** legal condition, that is ours whether we feel it or not. But this work of the Spirit is not like that at all. The Spirit brings us a radically **subjective** experience. What are its marks, its characteristics?

- First, the Spirit leads us to call out "Abba, Father". The Greek word *krazdon* is a very strong word that means a rending, loud cry. It refers to deep and profound passion and feeling.

- Second, "calls out" refers to our prayer life. Just as a child does not prepare speeches to his or her parents, so Christians experiencing this work of the Spirit find a great spontaneity and reality in prayer. Praying is no longer mechanical or formal, but filled with warmth, passion and freedom.

- Third, the phrase "calls out" connotes a sense of God's real presence. Just as a child calls out automatically to the nearby daddy when there's a problem or a question, so Christians experiencing this work of the Spirit feel the remarkable reality of nearness to God.

- Fourth, "Abba"—which is a babytalk word, meaning "Papa", or "Daddy"—signifies a confidence of love and assurance of welcome. Just as a young child simply assumes that a parent loves them and is there for them, and never doubts the security and openness of daddy's strong arms, so Christians can have an overwhelming boldness and certainty that God loves them endlessly.

The work of the *Son* is done externally to us, and is something we can have without feeling. But the work of the *Spirit* is done internally to us, and consists in us being completely moved—emotionally as well as intellectually—by the love of the Father. The work of Son and Spirit should never be divorced, nor one made to obscure the other. The fullness of the Spirit is experienced as we meditate on the love of the Son. The gifts of the Son are enjoyed as we look to the Spirit to guide us.

The Privileges of Sonship

What are the rights of sonship? "Because you are sons..." (**v 6**): we have intimacy of relationship, as we have seen in the previous section; and we have authority over possessions.

Sonship means we are each "an heir" (**v 7**). The only reason a servant would be adopted as a son would be because the father had no heir. So the person in Paul's illustration has a legal title to all the father's estate, because he is being treated as an only son.

So for a child of God, there is a confidence and boldness every day. We don't walk in fear of anyone or anything; our Father owns the place! God will honor us as He honors His one and only Son. We live with heads held high. Our sonship removes the fear of missing fulfillment or losing approval that is at the root of much of our disobedience.

> We don't walk in fear of anyone or anything: our Father owns the place!

And there is a guarantee of sharing God's glory in our future. The astonishing bottom line of sonship is that God now treats us as if we have done everything Jesus has done. We are treated as if we are "only sons", like Jesus. Jesus Himself said this as He prayed for His people: "Father … let the world know that you sent me and *have loved them even as you have loved me. Father, I want those you have given me to be with me where I am"* (John 17:21, 23-24).

Actually, all this is implied in the very use of the word "Abba" (**Galatians 4:6**). Why would Paul use an Aramaic idiomatic phrase in a letter to Greek-speaking Galatians, who probably didn't know Aramaic, the common language of Palestine? Because *Jesus Christ used it* in talking to His Father (Mark 14:36). It was a daringly familiar term to use to address the LORD Almighty. So when Paul says that we should use it, he is vividly asserting that we have legally inherited the rights of Jesus Himself. We can approach God as if we were as beautiful, heroic, and faithful as Jesus Himself. All that is His is ours.

So there are two specific steps we can take in order to have a deeper experience of our sonship. First, we must put aside significant time to study the work of the Son, asking the Spirit to illuminate us and make it real to us. The close connection of **verses 4-5** to **verses 6-7** means we must learn to meditate on the Bible; to connect our prayer to our study and our study to our prayer.

Second, we must "cry out" to our Father spontaneously, throughout the day. We must, in other words, analyze and address the issues of everyday life by remembering His fatherly love. We need to learn to ask, moment by moment: *Am I acting like a slave who is afraid of God, or like a child who is assured of my Father's love?* And as we cry "Abba, Father" in our lives, the Spirit does His work, assuring us "that we are God's children ... co-heirs with Christ" (Romans 8:16-17), and so flooding our hearts with life-changing assurance.

Questions for reflection

1. What has most excited you in this Bible section?

2. Is adoption something you *experience* as well as *understand?* How can you meditate on the Son's work more, and ask the Spirit to work on your affections more?

3. When are you most in danger of living as a slave, not a son?

8. TWO RELIGIONS, TWO MINISTRIES

These verses set before us two contrasts. One is between gospel faith and worldly religion (v 8-11), and is one of the most important and remarkable insights of the whole book. The other is between gospel ministry and worldly ministry (v 12-20), and gives us insights into how the gospel practically affects our relationships with others.

And it matters that we understand the contrasts, and learn to see them in our lives and around us. As Paul sees the Galatians failing to do this, he is in "fear for" and "perplexed about you" (**v 11, 20**).

The Idolatry of Biblical Religion

Many of the Galatian Christians had been worshipers at the idol-worshipping temples, and had lived the licentious and immoral lifestyles which went along with those religions. And unless we stop and think, verses 8-11 seem to be a warning to the Galatians not to go back to this kind of pagan idol-worship. After all, before they knew God, they were "slaves to those who by nature are not gods" (**v 8**). And now, Paul says: "you are turning back ... Do you wish to be enslaved by them all over again?" (**v 9**).

But then we remember that the whole point of Galatians is a warning not to adopt a *biblical legalism*. The false teachers were not encouraging the Gentile Christians to ignore God's law, as they had in their pagan days. Rather, they were urging them to adopt *all* the Old Testament Mosaic law, in order to be justified and pleasing to God (2:14-16).

Therefore, Paul is saying that earning one's own salvation through scrupulous biblical morality and religion is just as much enslavement to idols as outright paganism and all its immoral practices! In the end, the religious person is as lost and enslaved as the irreligious person.

> The religious person is as lost as the irreligious person.

Why? Both are trying to be their own savior and lord, but in different ways. Both are based on "the basic principles of the world" (v 3)—*stoichea tou cosmou,* the "principles" of **verse 9**, which Paul describes as "weak and miserable".

What does this term mean? Often, this word in ancient Greek referred to the elements of the material, visible world that make up nature: fire, water, air, and earth. This word also often referred to the pagan belief that spiritual forces or gods lay behind and worked through these elements to control people's lives and destinies. These beings had to be worshiped and appeased. So farmers sacrificed to a weather-god, lovers to the god of physical beauty, and so on.

In 1 Corinthians 8:4 and 10:19, Paul states boldly that there is no God but the true God. Zeus and Apollos and Poseidon don't exist. Yet then he immediately says: "But the sacrifices of pagans are offered to demons" (1 Corinthians 10:20). And he warns the Galatians that they can go back to being enslaved by these things that "by nature are not gods" (**Galatians 4:8**). Why? Because though the "gods" do not exist as such, we can become subject to enslavement by evil spiritual forces if we worship anything other than Jesus Christ.

The basic principle of the world is that we need to save ourselves. We will worship what we think we need to fulfill ourselves, to give us "life". And Paul is saying that any basic "thing"—money, sex, mountains and so on—can be worshiped, treated as a god, and become the basis of your religion. And whatever it is that we worship, we will be enslaved by.

For example, if we put our greatest hope in gaining wealth, we will be controlled and enslaved. We will be completely under the power of money. If we are not doing well at gaining it, we will be devastated. And even if we do get "enough", we will be disappointed, and seek more. If we treat things that are not gods as though they are, we become slaves to them spiritually.

So how can a turning to works-salvation be considered an enslavement to false gods? There are an infinite number of different ways that we can choose to earn our salvation through works, even if we don't think of it as earning our salvation at all. But whatever we choose to use, whether it is achievement or morality or religion or serving our family, we turn that thing into a savior, and thus into a "god". Works-righteousness always creates idols; it is simply that the false saviors it produces—church attendance, ministry to others, Bible-reading—are things we would not normally think of as idols.

We must feel the force of Paul's emphasis on "enslavement". If anything but Jesus is a requirement for being happy or worthy, that thing will become our slave master. Without the gospel, we *must* be under the slavery of an idol.

> Without the gospel, we *must* be under the slavery of an idol.

The perfect example of this is Jesus' story of the two brothers in Luke 15. A father had one very immoral, younger, **prodigal** son, and one very moral elder son. Both of them wanted control of the father's wealth but did not want the father. Both were alienated from the father's heart. At the end of the story though, the immoral son repents and goes in to the father, while the moral one stays outside in anger.

If anything, the idolatry and slavery of religion is more dangerous than the idolatry and slavery of irreligion, because it is less obvious. The irreligious person knows he is far away from God, but the religious person does not.

This is why Paul is in "fear for" the Galatians. They were taking on "special days and months and seasons and years" (**v 10**)—they were (literally) religiously observing all the festivals and ceremonies of the Old Testament. And this new slavery to "non-gods" would be worse than the old. They would not know they were far away from the Father.

The Assurance of Being "Known"

It is easy to miss, but in **verse 9** Paul points the Galatians back to a right relationship with the Father. He makes a comparison between being a slave to an impersonal and nonexistent idol-"god" (**v 8**) and knowing relationally the true God. But then he seems to correct himself: "now that you know God—or rather are known by God" (**v 9**).

Paul isn't saying they don't know God. Anyone who has eternal life knows God (John 17:3), and Paul does not question that they have "put on Christ" (Galatians 3:27). The word "rather" probably means "more importantly". Paul is saying: *How can you turn back to idols since you know God and, more importantly, are known by God?!*

What makes a person a Christian is not so much your knowing God but His knowing of you. "To know" in the Bible means more than intellectual awareness. To know someone is to enter into a personal relationship with him or her. *So then,* Paul says, *it's not so much your regard and love for God, but rather His regard and love of you, that really makes you a Christian.* Paul says in 1 Corinthians 8:3 that anyone who loves God does so because God knows them. That is, He has set His love on us in Jesus. Our knowing of God will rise and fall depending on many things. But God's knowing of us is absolutely fixed and solid.

Why is this an antidote to idolatry? Because, as Richard Lovelace says:

"Christians who are no longer sure that God loves and accepts them in Jesus, apart from their present spiritual achievements, are subconsciously radically insecure persons, much less secure than non-Christians, because of the constant bulletins they receive from their Christian environment about the holiness of God and the righteousness they are supposed to have. Their insecurity shows itself in pride, a fierce defensive assertion of their own righteousness and defensive criticism of others. They cling desperately to legal, pharisaical righteousness, but envy [and] jealousy and other ... sin grow out of their fundamental insecurity." (*Dynamics of Spiritual Life*, pages 211-212)

So it is our insecurity regarding our acceptance with God which is the reason we make idols. We look at our knowing of Him (which fluctuates so much) instead of His knowing of us in Christ. We are desperately trying to firm up a positive self-image by using our idols.

Paul reminds us that the gospel shows us we don't need to make ourselves beautiful or lovable to God; He already knows us. If this is the case, we don't need to make an idol out of other people's approval or even our own self-approval.

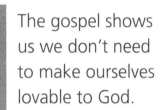

The gospel shows us we don't need to make ourselves lovable to God.

The classic statement of this is in 1 Corinthians 4:3-4. There Paul says that not only does he not care about other people's evaluation of him, he does not even care for his own evaluation of himself. Rather, all that counts is God's evaluation or "judgment" of him.

But all of the letter to the Galatians is about how, in Jesus Christ, God's judgment is that we are justified; we are regarded by God as wholly perfect and righteous. So when we put Galatians next to 1 Corinthians 4, we see that Paul's view of himself is to say: *Since God knows me, and sees Christ when He looks at me, I don't care what you think about me, and I don't even care what I think.*

The great and central basis of Christian assurance is not how much our hearts are set on God, but how unshakably His heart is set on us.

And if we begin to grasp that we are "known by God", we won't seek to bolster our self-image or standing before Him through our works. We won't worship any idol—we will love Him, the One who knows us.

How do we grasp this? The nineteenth-century missionary to China, Hudson Taylor, had a scrap of paper which he would move in his diary each day, so that whatever else he was doing in his day, he would always read this:

Lord Jesus, make Thyself to me a living bright reality.
More present to faith's vision keen than any outward objects seem.
More dear, more intimately nigh, than e'en the sweetest earthly tie.

If we know Jesus, and know that He knows us, we will enjoy Him, and push the controlling idols aside.

Questions for reflection

1. What idols are you in most danger of serving?

2. How does God knowing you reassure you today?

3. How does remembering that God knows you free you from the temptation to worship idols?

PART TWO

Gospel Ministry

Paul was a man who poured himself into his ministry. And while the first two autobiographical chapters of his letter refer to a time before he came to Galatia, in 4:12-20 we're given an insight into how he planted a church there. As he does so, Paul is looking back on a time when his gospel ministry flourished in Galatia, and when the relationships between him and the young Christians there were healthy. So there is much for us to learn here about gospel ministry and relationships in our settings today.

First, gospel ministry is *culturally flexible:* "I became like you" (**v 12**). A ministry that's energized by the gospel is flexible and adaptable with *everything* apart from the gospel. It is not tied to every specific of culture and custom. Its leaders can come and truly live among the people they are seeking to reach and adopt their ways and love them.

One of the marks of a legalistic, works-righteous mindset is that it is inflexible, and obsessed with details. Such a person wants the converts to dress and act "just like us". Paul, on the other hand, is a model of someone who truly comes close to and enters into the lives of the people he is seeking to reach—just as Christ did in His incarnation. Paul not only got to know them personally, but he lived with them, ate with them, played with them, talked and walked with them. He got to know their world and lived in it appreciatively, even though it was not his world. He entered in as far as he could to their questions and problems, their hopes and fears and sensitivities, and adapted his life and speech and message to them without, of course, changing the gospel itself.

> A ministry that's energized by the gospel is flexible and adaptable with everything apart from the gospel.

Second, gospel ministry is *transparent:* "Become like me" (**v 12**). Paul has been so personally open about his own heart and so consistent in his own life that he can invite the Galatians to imitate him.

Our words are not sufficient for (and maybe not even most important in) persuading others about the truth of Christ. People have to be able to look into our hearts and lives, to assess how we handle trouble, how we deal with disappointment and interruptions, how we conduct our relationships, how we feel and act, so that they can see whether Christ is real and how the gospel affects a day-to-day human life. Generally, we find faith mainly through relationships with joyful, flawed-but-honest, loving Christians, not through arguments, information and books.

This is not arrogance. If Paul had only said: "Be like me" without becoming "like them", then this would be an indicator of pride. But Paul is not urging them to be as *right* as he is, but as *joyful* as he is.

Third, gospel ministry looks for *opportunities in hardship.* Problems become possibilities. "It was because of an illness," he reminds the Galatians, "that I first preached the gospel to you" (**v 13**). That most likely means he was in Galatia either because of a detour from his planned itinerary or because of a delay in his planned schedule. Either way, he was not planning on preaching the gospel to them. But the illness caused it to happen.

> Gospel ministry looks for opportunities in hardship.

God and Suffering

We need to take a diversion here, because we are being confronted with one of the most challenging and most troubling parts of Christian teaching, namely that God allows the suffering and difficulties of the world into the lives of Christians. Romans 8:28 insists that "in all things [pleasant and painful] God works for the good of those who love him". In this case, hundreds of lives were changed because God allowed a painful illness to overtake Paul. And here we also have an example of how God thwarted well-laid plans in order to bring enormous good, though through suffering.

God does not promise to bless Christians by removing suffering, but to bless Christians through suffering. Jesus suffered not so that we might not suffer, but so that in our suffering we would become like Him. God uses our suffering to bring about good. Sometimes this involves circumstances—Paul's illness brought him many new friends and a successful ministry in Galatia—but other times the "good" God works is in our character.

> God does not promise to bless us by removing suffering, but to bless us through suffering.

In 2 Corinthians 12:7-10, Paul talks about a great, unnamed, painful "thorn" which God would not remove despite repeated prayers. But Paul says that the "thorn" is meant for good because it has humbled him (v 7—"to keep me from being conceited") and it has strengthened him (v 9—"that Christ's power may rest on me"). The relentless pain and sense of weakness (whatever its cause) has brought Paul to a deeper dependence on and vision of the sufficiency of grace (v 9): "My grace [ie: my unmerited love for you] is sufficient for you."

This is also a great reminder that ministry does not happen strictly according to human plan. Paul had not targeted Galatia in his strategic planning sessions, but God brought him there. Now, we cannot infer from this text that strategic planning is wrong; Paul did not repent and stop making plans for his missionary journeys! We see, for example, that he continued to target the largest cities of every region as a way to reach the region.

We must use the wisdom that we have to make plans. We must be stewards of our time and resources, and must plan to use them in the way that seems to best produce fruit. But this does teach that we must be very relaxed and willing to let God edit our plans greatly.

When we begin a Bible study for certain people, we may find a whole different set of people being reached. When we advertise an event, we may find that most of the people whose lives are changed came by some strange coincidence or by some very remote chance conversation with a stranger, etc.

Most of us can provide personal illustrations of how God worked in our lives or the lives around us through mistakes, "disasters", troubles, and thwarted plans, often far more than through our deliberate actions and goals.

An Enemy?

The Galatians had received Paul very warmly. It would have been very easy to have treated him with "contempt and scorn"; perhaps because his illness was disfiguring. Instead, they welcomed him "as if I were an angel of God, as if I were Christ Jesus himself" (**v 14**). But now we have a great change. The joy and satisfaction they used to feel for him is gone: "What has happened to all your joy?" (**v 15**). Now they have begun to see Paul as a hostile agent. When he says: "Have I now become your enemy?" (**v 15**), he means they are now beginning to treat him as an adversary. There has been alienation over the doctrines of faith and good works at issue in the letter. As he has been telling them "the truth", their friendship has cooled drastically.

Why does Paul include verses 12-16? To show them that though he has not changed in his message or his ministry, the church's response to him has—since they are now under the influence of ministers who have a very different message from his, because they have very different goals and means.

Two Goals of Two Ministries

The false teachers' goal is "that you may be zealous for them" (**v 17**). The NIV misses some of the nuances of Paul's sentence. The phrase "zealous to win you over" renders a word that means literally "to build up" or even "puff up". It translates better as: *They are flattering and making much of you, so that you will flatter and make much of them.*

A gospel-energized ministry does not need to have fans who are emotionally dependent on the leaders. It seeks to please God, assured of salvation through faith. These false teachers, on the other hand, are ministering not because they are sure of their salvation but in order to be sure of and win their salvation. Just as they are calling the Galatians to earn their salvation through works, so they are earning their salvation through works—it is salvation-by-ministry.

This means that they need, emotionally, to have people who emotionally need them. They need their converts and their disciples to be wrapped up in their leaders, obeying and adoring them. Only this can assure them that they are good and great believers, truly blessed and favored by God.

> False teachers need to have people who need them.

This goal affects the means they use. They are "zealous to win you over" (**v 17**). This is a way of saying: *They are telling you what you want to hear; they are tickling your ears, pandering to you in order to get your loyalty.* There is nothing wrong with **zeal** (**v 18**) in itself; what dictates whether zeal is good or bad is whether "the purpose is good". The false teachers simply want to be built up by building the Galatians up—not in the gospel, but in pride and self-righteousness.

By contrast, Paul's goal is in **verse 19**: he is in agony "until Christ be formed in you". This is very critical. Despite Paul's appeal in **verse 12** to "become like me", Paul is only being an example to the Galatians in order for them to be changed into the likeness of Christ. Paul does not say "like me", but "become like me". He is not trying to get fans but to get people to follow Christ as he does. Paul wants people not to become dependent on him, but on Christ.

This is why Paul uses the image of labor here. He is like a mother, laboring "in the pains of childbirth" over his disciples. A mother in labor desperately wants her child to get out and be independently alive! A child grows inside the mother. The mother must suffer in order to give life to the child, but that does not mean she wants the child to stay in the womb. It's a remarkable image for healthy, gospel-based ministry.

The false teachers want followers who glorify them; Paul wants partners who glorify Christ. And that directs the means to his goal. Unlike his opponents, Paul is not telling the Galatians what they would like to hear. He is telling them "the truth" (**v 16**), and he is being vilified for it. Paul would love to be able to be affirming and gentle, to be able to "change my tone" (**v 20**). But he would rather hold out the gospel than receive the praise. After all, it is the gospel which brings people to Christ-dependence, shapes people in Christ-likeness, and provokes people to Christ-praise.

> Paul would rather hold out the gospel than receive the praise.

The gospel frees us from the need for people's approval and adoration so that we can confront and anger the people we love if that is what is best for them. And although it does not always work, this is the only kind of communication that really changes people. If you love a person so selfishly that you cannot risk their anger, you won't ever tell them the truth they need to hear. If, on the other hand, you tell a person the truth they need, but with harshness and not with the agony of a lover, they won't listen to it.

But if you speak the truth with lots of love evident at the same time, there is a great chance that what you say will penetrate the heart and heal. A gospel-based ministry is marked by loving honesty, not spin, image and flattery.

This kind of gospel ministry is costly to the minister. It is not always easy for those they are ministering to. But it is based on the truth; it is pointing to Christ; and it is eternally worthwhile. We would do well to imitate Paul in our ministry to others; and to love and thank those who love us enough to minister to us as he did to the Galatians.

Questions for reflection

1. What has particularly struck you about the nature and conduct of true gospel ministry?

2. Do you ever find it appealing to have people relying on you in some way? Why? Could you be motivated by the same goals as the false teachers?

3. We can all be gospel ministers to fellow Christians. How will your ministry change, based on this Bible section?

9. GRACE TO THE BARREN

These verses are explosive. They round off the themes Paul has been highlighting since the middle of chapter 2. His point here is not only that the gospel makes absolutely anyone a child of God, but that the most proud and moral and religiously "able" are often the ones left out of God's family. The gospel reverses the world's values.

Four Types of People

Paul is now directly addressing "you who want to be under the law" (**v 21**). He is (so to speak) looking straight in the eyes of those Galatian Christians who have become convinced that they need to add their performance to Christ's if they are to be acceptable to God.

As we've seen before (*page 42*), Paul does not mean *obeying* the law here. To be "under the law" means *relying on* the law for your standing with God. And so this is a message that will particularly challenge religious people; as John Stott wrote:

"There are many such today. They are not Judaizers to whom Paul was writing, but people whose religion is legalistic, who imagine that the way to God is by observance of certain rules."

(*The Message of Galatians*, page 122)

It is helpful to see that there are four kinds of people in the world:

1. *Law-obeying, law-relying.* These people are under the law, and are usually very smug, self-righteous and superior. Externally, they are very sure they are right with God, but deep down, they have a lot of insecurity, since no one can truly be assured that they are living up to the standard. This makes them touchy, sensitive to criticism and devastated when their prayers aren't answered. This includes members of other religions, but here I am thinking mainly of people who go to church. These people have much in common with the **Pharisees** of Jesus' day.

2. *Law-disobeying, law-relying.* These people have a religious conscience of strong works-righteousness, but they are not living consistently with it. As a result of this, they are more humble and more tolerant of others than the "Pharisees" above, but they are also much more guilt-ridden, subject to mood swings and sometimes very afraid of religious topics. Some of these people may go to church, but they stay on the periphery because of their low spiritual self-esteem.

3. *Law-disobeying, not law-relying.* These are the people who have thrown off the concept of the law of God. They are intellectually secular or **relativistic**, or have a very vague spirituality. They largely choose their own moral standards and then insist that they are meeting them. But Paul, in Romans 1:18-20, says that at a sub-conscious level, they know there is a God who they should be obeying. Such people are usually happier and more tolerant than either of the above groups. But usually there is a strong, liberal self-righteousness. They are earning their own salvation by feeling superior to others. It is just that this is usually a less obvious kind of self-righteousness.

4. *Law-obeying, not law-relying.* These are Christians who understand the gospel and are living out of the freedom of it. They obey the law of God out of grateful joy that comes from the knowledge of their sonship, and out of freedom from the fear and selfishness that false idols had generated. They are more tolerant than number 3, more sympathetic than number 1, and more confident than number 2. But most Christians struggle to live out number 4, and tend to see the world as a #1, #2, or even #3 person. But to the degree that they do, they are impoverished spiritually.

Under the Law? Listen to the Law!

The question in **verse 21** is designed to show law-reliers that their position undermines itself. They want to be under the law—but if they were "aware of what the law [actually] says" (**v 21**), then they wouldn't want to be under it anymore! Paul is saying: *The very law you say that you follow contradicts you.*

The word "law" was often used to mean the Old Testament as a whole; the record of the will of God. So Paul is going back to the story of Hagar and Sarah, which likely was used by the false teachers, who told the Galatians: *You are not really children of Abraham unless you obey all the law of Moses.*

Paul is turning the tables on them by reminding them that: "Abraham had two sons, one by the slave woman and the other by the free woman" (**v 22**). Therefore there are two ways of being related to Abraham: one right way and one wrong way.

It is a brilliant argument. The basic point of the false teachers was: *Yes, it is good that you believe in Christ, but you will have to obey the whole law before you can be considered the children of Abraham.* Paul's basic point is: *The moment you believed in Christ, you were the children of Abraham, the heirs of all the promises of God! And the moment you start thinking you have to obey the whole law, you are not the children of Abraham at all!*

Learning from Hagar

Abraham had two sons, Ishmael and Isaac, by two different women. And they were born in very different circumstances, which are crucial to understanding the point Paul is making.

God had promised that He would provide Abraham with an heir to live in the land that God would show Abraham (Genesis 12:1-4; 15:4-5). But he was old, his wife Sarah was barren, and he had lived in this land for a decade without children. So Sarah suggested that Abraham sleep with her maidservant, Hagar, so they could "build a family through her" (16:1-2). "Abraham agreed", Hagar conceived (v 4), and Ishmael was born (v 15).

Fourteen years later, when Abraham was one hundred, he had another child, this time by his barren wife. "The LORD did for Sarah what he had promised. Sarah became pregnant and bore a son to Abraham in his old age … Abraham gave the name Isaac to the son Sarah bore him" (Genesis 21:1-3—notice the narrator's repetition of "Sarah"; he wants to make very clear to the reader that Isaac is the son of Sarah, the barren, childless woman!). Paul sums up the differences in births when he says: "[The] son by the slave woman was born in the ordinary way; but his son by the free woman was born as the result of a promise" (**Galatians 4:23**).

Abraham knew that he would have a child who would be his heir and the bearer of the line which would bring salvation into the world. But how could this son be born? Sarah was a barren woman and very old, and it would take an extraordinary, supernatural act of God for a son to come that way. On the other hand, the maidservant Hagar was young and fertile. By the customs of the time, it would be perfectly legal to have a son through her (though it would not be according to God's will, see Genesis 2:24).

Abraham decided not to wait on God's supernatural actions to get his son. Instead, he decided to get his son through human attainment, through what he was capable of and what Hagar was capable of.

The Controversial Reversal

Jews knew that they were the children of Abraham, descended from him through Isaac, and heirs of God's promises. Their ancestors had received God's law at Mount Sinai; their nation was centered on Jerusalem and its temple.

The false teachers were telling the Gentile Galatian Christians that to be true children of Abraham, inheritors of the promises, they needed to *become Jewish*.

Paul's words in **verses 24-25** are incendiary! Look who he aligns Hagar with: "The women represent two covenants. One covenant is from Mount Sinai and bears children who are to be slaves: This is Hagar. Now Hagar stands for Mount Sinai in Arabia and corresponds to the present city of Jerusalem."

Paul says clearly that Hagar and her son, Ishmael, represent the law covenant of Sinai and the earthly city of Jerusalem, which by and large consists of persons who have not accepted Christ. And these people are "in slavery" (**v 25**), because they are under law. Paul is linking several things together: the **Sinai covenant of law**; the present Jerusalem; Hagar; and all who make the law the means of justification with God and the main principle of life.

This has been Paul's point throughout chapters 3 and 4, but he has now brilliantly and dramatically made his point afresh, through a stunning link to Hagar and Sarah. We'll look at the latter in a moment, but Paul wanted those who were listening to the false teachers to feel the full force of his insight that Hagar, not Sarah, "corresponds to the present city of Jerusalem" (**v 25**).

By sleeping with Hagar, Abraham was choosing to rely on his own capabilities. He was opting to "work" and gain his son. He was acting in faith: but the faith he had was in himself, as his own "savior".

The immediate result was disaster! Sarah became terribly jealous of Hagar and the family was wracked with division and sadness (Genesis 16:4-14; 21:8-21). This is not surprising, since the Bible uniformly condemns **polygamy** and having **concubines.** And here, God (although He looked after Hagar and Ishmael—16:7-12; 21:17-18) never directed His promises through this son of Abraham—Abraham's bid for self-salvation failed.

> By sleeping with Hagar, Abraham was acting in faith: faith in himself.

As history went on, strife and warfare between the descendants of Isaac and Ishmael continued. Ishmael is traditionally the father of the Arab peoples; so Paul refers to "Mount Sinai in Arabia" (**v 25**): law-reliers ("Mount Sinai"), who are outside God's people ("Arabia"). Isaac was the father of the Jews.

Abraham did not rely on God's grace through His supernatural action in history but rather on his own ability. When we fail to rest in God and instead seek to be our own savior, the result is havoc and disintegration—spiritually, psychologically, and relationally.

Though the false teachers proudly consider themselves related to Abraham by Sarah and Isaac, Paul says that they are spiritually descended from the slave woman, the Gentile, the outcast. Their heart and approach to God is like Abraham with Hagar, and the fruit in their lives is like Ishmael—just more slavery! Though racially they are from Sarah, in their soul and heart they are like the people they despise.

They rely on their own ability rather than the supernatural grace of God. The most religious people can be furthest from freedom.

Questions for reflection

1. Look back over your past and trace your spiritual life in terms of the four categories on pages 117-118.

2. Abraham decided to rely on himself to make God's promises come to pass. Have you ever done something similar? What were the results?

3. When have you seen God do what seems impossible in your own life, or in the lives of those around you?

PART TWO

An Allegory of the Gospel

Paul is using the story of Abraham, Hagar and Sarah only as an **allegory**. Some people are disturbed that Hagar (who in the actual story is an innocent victim) represents something negative in Galatians 4, while Sarah (who in the actual story is an unbelieving collaborator with Abraham) represents something positive. But we must remember that Paul himself says: "These things may be taken figuratively" (**v 24**). In other words, though we must read the account as a literally true story and learn the theological and moral lessons of it, that is not what Paul is doing here. He finds the story to be a good, symbolic illustration of grace and works. It's not that he doesn't think it is historical. But he wants to use it as an illustration of a biblical truth. And, as we've seen, he wants to use it to turn the tables on his opponents.

Taken in this narrow, figurative sense, Hagar's son represents seeking salvation by works, and Sarah relying on salvation by God's grace.

This is a really interesting analogy. The gospel is that we do not try to attain a righteousness that our abilities can develop. Rather, we are to receive a righteousness provided through supernatural acts of God in history—the miraculous birth, sin-bearing death, and death-defeating resurrection of Christ. We need to rely on God—just as Abraham eventually learned that he needed the miraculous work of God to provide him with a son and heir. As Abraham needed to switch his faith from his own efforts to God's supernatural work, so these Galatian Christians need to look back to Christ's work, rather than at their own law-keeping efforts.

So Sarah, "the free woman", whose son was "born as a result of a promise" (**v 23**), has nothing

> The Galatians need to look back to Christ, rather than at their own efforts.

to do with the earthly, grace-rejecting Jerusalem, but "the Jerusalem that is above [that] is free". In the sense that she stands for those who have learned to cease trying to attain salvation and have learned to allow God to save them, "she is our mother" (**v 26**). Your "mother-city" was the place where you were at home, a citizen, with rights.

So Sarah = heaven = the Christian's mother. Heaven, right now, is our home, where the Christian belongs.

The Gospel: Grace to the Barren

Paul now shows that the gospel of "grace to the barren" does not spring only from his figurative reading of Hagar and Sarah; it is the gospel which runs right through the Old Testament Scriptures. So in **verse 27** he quotes Isaiah 54:1: "More are the children of the desolate woman than of her who has a husband".

Originally this prophetic word was for the Jewish exiles in Babylon, around 1200 years after Abraham's time, and 600 years before Paul's. The remaining Israelites thought their national life was over, that they would never return home, or have their own country again. They seemed like failures, weak and helpless (their exile was a punishment), while other nations seemed strong and able. But God says to them, through Isaiah: *Now that you are helpless, you will see that it is the weak in whose lives my grace works! The strong are too busy relying on themselves. I will make you numerous and great.*

The prophecy of Isaiah looks back to Genesis 16, in which God looks down on two women, one beautiful and fertile, the other barren and old, and He chooses to save the world through the barren one.

And through her family would come another unlikely son, born to another woman who could have no expectation of being pregnant, not because she was barren but because she was a virgin. And through *that* Son, all the peoples of the world would be blessed, just as God promised Abraham and Sarah. That is how God's grace works.

Now Paul takes up the same story that Isaiah used, and gives it an even more full and wonderful application. The Galatians are being "beaten up", spiritually speaking, by the false teachers. They are being told that they are too polluted and flawed simply to consider themselves loved children of God the moment they believe. But now Paul turns the tables and comforts the Galatians powerfully. They are the "barren woman." If salvation is by works, then only the "fertile" can have "children". Only the morally able and strong, the people from good families, the folk with good records can be spiritually fruitful, enjoy the love and joy of God and transform the lives of others.

But if the gospel is true, it does not matter who you are or who you were. You may be a spiritual and moral outcast, as marginal as the single, barren woman was in those ancient days. It does not matter. You will bear fruit, the kind that lasts.

The gospel says: *Grace is not just for fertile Hagars, but for barren Sarahs. If Sarah can have a future, anyone can!*

> If the gospel is true, it does not matter who you are or who you were.

In fact it goes deeper even than this, because Paul is saying that the gospel of grace is *especially* for the barren. The able and the "fertile" think they can attain without God, and so they reject the gospel of grace. Paul is saying what Jesus says in the **parable** of the prodigal and elder brothers in Luke 15. The gospel shows us that it is the "strong", moral, good, religious, and self-righteous who, in the end, are the slaves.

The Gospel for Disappointed Failures

Sarah is a huge encouragement for those who see themselves as failures. In those ancient times, a woman's worth essentially consisted entirely in her ability to bear children. Of course, this is not something the Bible condoned. In fact, this very passage completely undermines the terrible mistake that so many societies make. Ancient cultures told a woman that her worth and "righteousness" were her ability to produce children, and that if she could not bear children, her life was useless to the tribe. (To a great degree, even in our modern society, single or childless women often feel very stigmatized and useless, being given an unspoken suggestion that they have failed in some way.)

But the Bible shows us here that we should not make children our life and worth any more than we should make career or money or power or approval our worth. The gospel cries out that the people who have most will find that their false strategies of self-worth collapse—and the "barren, the poor, the marginal" can be more fruitful, rich, and powerful than all the rest. They can bear great fruit if they begin to live out the gospel and serve others.

> The people who have most will find their false strategies of self-worth collapse.

The pastor of a church in Harlem, whose membership is mostly black, once told me how over 80 years ago their congregation was founded by a German lady who lived in Manhattan. She was a dedicated Christian, and through her Bible study, two African-American women from Harlem came to Christ. They asked her to begin a ministry up in Harlem to reach more of their friends.

The German lady was engaged at the time, and her fiancé was very much against her doing such a ministry. He said he would call off the wedding if she went. As she agonized between the call she felt from God and her desire to be married, she came upon Isaiah 54:1: "More are the children of the desolate woman than of her who has a husband". She followed God's call, lost her fiancé, and the new church was born which today is Bethel Gospel. She had, and has, far more spiritual children than any physical ones her lost marriage would have given. This is just one example of the principle.

Religion and philosophy in general say that God and salvation are only for those who are good. That's an exclusive message. Now, the gospel is also exclusive. It says that God and salvation are only for those who know they are not good. But the gospel has a far more inclusive exclusivity! Anyone can belong to God through the gospel, regardless of record and background, regardless of who you have been or what you have done or how weak you are. Rule-keeping religion is for the noble, the able, the moral, the strong, but the gospel is for anyone. Jesus actually said that the able, moral and strong are in general farther from the kingdom than the moral failures and the spiritually weak.

This is the message of Jesus' lesser-known parable about two sons, which he tells to "the chief priests and elders of the people" (Matthew 21:23). One is told by his father to work in his vineyard, refuses, but later changes his mind (v 28-29). The other says he will, but never actually goes to the vineyard (v 30). It's the first son, not the second, who actually does what the father wanted. The point? "The tax collectors and the prostitutes are entering the kingdom of God ahead of you" (v 31). Why? Because "you did not repent and believe" (v 32).

This is why everyone, from the most religious to the most non-religious, needs the gospel of grace. Religious people are rejecting Jesus as Savior, because all their religious works are efforts to merit God's favor. Their savior is their own achievements; Jesus may be an example or a helper, but He is not Savior.

But non-religious people are worshiping something, too. All of us need a sense of worth or value. So everyone has a worshipful faith in something from which they must derive that value. But these things control us as we

> Everyone, from the most religious to the most non-religious, needs the gospel of grace.

seek them, disappoint us if we find them, and devastate us if we lose them.

So in our natural state, the motives for both serving God and rejecting God are identical. In both cases we seek to maintain independence from God by denying that we are so sinful that we needed to be saved totally by grace. Instead, we seek to earn our own value. We are "Ishmaels"; and Ishmaels are always in bondage. That is what self-reliance always leads to. Only "Isaacs"—"children of promise" (**v 28**)—live in freedom.

How Ishmaels Treat Isaacs

There is one more surprise in these verses. Paul draws a final lesson from Ishmael and Isaac: "at that time the son born in the ordinary way persecuted the son born by the power of the Spirit" (**v 29**—see Genesis 21:8-9). And "it is the same now", in first-century Galatia.

Paul is flatly stating that the children of the slave—those seeking salvation through law-obedience—will always persecute the children of the free woman, those enjoying salvation-by-grace. Ishmaels will persecute Isaacs.

Why is this? Because the gospel is more threatening to religious people than non-religious people. Religious people are very touchy and nervous about their standing with God. Their insecurity makes them hostile to the gospel, which insists that their best deeds are useless before God. One of the ways we know that our self-image is based on justification by Christ is that we are not hateful and hostile to people who differ from us; one of the ways we know that our self-image is based on justification by works is that we persecute!

So Ishmael laughed at Isaac. The Lord Jesus was most bitterly opposed by the religious leaders and was condemned by His own nation. In Galatia, the persecution was not physical, but it was no less dangerous; it was law-reliant teachers within the church undermining gospel freedom. It is the same today, as John Stott describes:

"The persecution of the true church ... is not always by the world, who are strangers ... but by our half-brothers, religious people, the nominal church. The greatest enemies of evangelical faith today are not unbelievers ... but the church, the establishment, the hierarchy. Isaac is always mocked and persecuted by Ishmael." (*The Message of Galatians*, page 127)

Questions for reflection

1. Can you identify with Sarah in any way? If you can, how does her experience comfort and excite you?

2. In what ways could you treat children (either those you have, or those you don't) as your savior?

3. How would you use this passage to answer the objection: "The Christian message is exclusive"?

10. GOSPEL FREEDOM

We've seen Paul (repeatedly!) telling the Galatians that Christians need not fear any condemnation because of their failure to keep the law, because they are righteous in Christ. When many people hear this, they say: *Boy! If I believed that, I'd be able to live any way I wanted!*

At first sight, the gospel seems to remove all incentive to live a holy life. This is why, over the centuries, churches have felt the need to tone down the radical claims of the gospel, trading gospel freedom for a message which aims to stop people living "any way I want".

So this is a critical passage. Paul wants to show us that gospel freedom from fear and condemnation leads us to obey God, not to please ourselves.

Set free for freedom

Verse 1 is the summary of the last two chapters of the book (and, in a sense, of the whole of the book). First, Paul tells us that we have a profound freedom in Christ. Paul's initial sentence is even stronger and more emphatic in Greek than how it comes across in English. He literally says: "For freedom Christ freed you". Both the noun and the verb are the word "freedom"; freedom is both the means and the end of the Christian life! Everything about the Christian gospel is freedom. Jesus' whole mission was an operation of liberation. And the verb translated "has set us free" is in the **aorist tense**. In Greek this refers to a single, past action that is now completed.

So, in the most definitive way, Paul tells us that Christians have been set free.

Yet second, he warns that this freedom we have in the gospel can be lost. It is important that Paul mentions this, because the emphatic, triumphant declaration of the first half of **verse 1** might lead us to believe this gospel freedom is so great and strong that it can't be lost. Paul says, though, that despite its divine source, our freedom is fragile and can slip from our grasp.

> Despite its divine source, our freedom is fragile and can slip from our grasp.

There are two implications (at least!) of these two points. First, to keep our freedom we must "stand firm". There is an interesting parallel here with political freedom. It is a well-observed fact that it takes vigilance and responsibility for a nation or group of people to maintain their political independence. Paul says that this is just as true with regard to this spiritual freedom. Free believers need to stand firm in their freedom (see also 1 Corinthians 16:13; Philippians 1:27; 4:1). To "stand firm" is essentially a military word, mixing together the ideas of keeping alert, being strong, resisting attack and sticking together.

In short, despite the fact that we already have been saved by Christ, we must be continually diligent to remember, preserve, rejoice in and live in accord with our salvation. We cannot lose our salvation, but we can lose our freedom from enslavement to fear.

The second implication looks back to the radical truth in Galatians 4 that we have already discussed, that law-keeping religion is really slavery. Paul exhorts them not to become "burdened ... by a **yoke**" (**v 1**). It was common in Judaism of the time to talk about taking on the study and practice of the whole law of Moses as coming under the "yoke". But both Christ and the early church saw the Pharisees and teachers of the law as enslaving people with this yoke (see Acts 15:10; compare Matthew 11:29-30).

The Galatians were in danger of going under this yoke. But the startling word in this last sentence is the word "again". The Galatian Christians had been pagans, who were under the slavery of literal idolatry—"the basic principles of the world" (4:3, 8-9). But here Paul once more makes his radical claim that pagan idolatry and biblical moralism (ie: keeping the laws of the Bible) are basically the same thing. The Galatians had been **amoral** liberals, and now they were about to become very moral conservatives.

Paul is saying that these boil down to the same spiritual slavery! Under circumcision, the Galatians will experience once again the anxiety, guilt and burdened life they knew before as pagans. They will never be sure that they are being good *enough*. Their lives will be as fear-based and proud and guilt-ridden as they were before; in fact, probably more so! They will fall into the touchiness, insecurity, pride, discouragement and weariness of people who are never sure that they have worth (ie: righteousness).

When Christ has no Value

Ultimately, the Galatians face an either-or decision. Will they make Christ their treasure, in whom they find their forgiveness and fulfillment; or will they look to law-keeping, to circumcision?

The teaching of the Judaizers was: *Unless you are circumcised and keep the law, you cannot be saved* (see Acts 15:1, 5). Paul retorts that, on the contrary, if they adopt this teaching and follow it, then they cannot be saved: "Christ will be of no value" (**v 2**) to them.

Again, we see Paul repeating a point he has made earlier in this letter (in this case, in chapter 1). So again, we need to remember that Scripture repeats itself for a purpose: because we need to listen, and go on listening!

And Paul wants the Galatians to remember that you can't add to Christ without subtracting Christ. He is either all their value, or He is without value. If law-obedience becomes part of their system of salvation, it is their *only* system, so they are "required to obey the whole law" (**v 3**); which, as we've seen, is simply impossible (3:10-11). Justification through law is self-salvation; it is to be "**alienated** from Christ" (**v 4**). We cannot hold on to grace if we are living by works (**v 4**).

> We cannot hold on to grace if we are living by works.

In short, **verse 1** reminds us of our subjective freedom in Christ; that we are no longer obeying God under a burdened, enslaved motivation. **Verses 2-4** remind us of our objective freedom in Christ; that we are freed from the obligation to obey the whole law in order to be justified before God. Paul is saying that the gospel frees us from both the guilt and slavery of sin, from both the condemnation of sin and the motivation to sin.

Does **verse 4** mean that real Christians can lose their salvation, can truly fall away from grace? It can appear that way. But, as we will see immediately below (**v 5-6**), Christians base their whole lives on the assurance and certainty of their present and future acceptance with God. Assurance of salvation is not possible if we think we must earn or even maintain our salvation by our efforts. If we keep ourselves saved by good living, how could we ever be sure we were being good enough to retain God's favor? Yet the Bible often says that we Christians can know we are safe and saved (eg: 1 John 2:3). In other words, we didn't earn our salvation by our behavior, and we can't "un-earn" it by our behavior.

John says of anyone who turns their back on the faith permanently: "They were not of us, for if they had been of us, they would have continued with us." (1 John 2:19, ESV). His point is that true Christians are saved by grace, and show they are Christians by continuing to trust in grace! Equally, those who fall away from grace never really trusted in it! This is why Paul is able to say in **verse 10:** "I am confident in the Lord that you will take no other view"—he believes that they are real Christians, and so their positive response to his warning will show that they do believe the gospel from the heart.

But Christians still need to hear the warning of **verses 2-4**. Paul is saying: *No matter that you insist you've been converted or you say you feel Christ has changed your life. If by deciding your salvation rests in any way on your performance, you deny salvation by faith alone in Christ alone (which I'm confident you won't), you can't be saved by Him.* He is saying that this is an acid test of whether someone is a Christian or not.

Hoping for What we Have

Instead of striving for righteousness—an effort which is doomed to failure—Paul encourages the Galatians to simply "await … the righteousness for which we hope" (**v 5**).

The biblical word *elpida*, translated "hope", does not have the much weaker meaning that it has in English. In the Bible, "hope" does not mean "hope so", as in: *"Will it be sunny tomorrow?" "I hope so (but I have no way of being confident it will be so)"*. It means a powerful assurance and certainty of something (see Hebrews 11:1).

This is a major problem for the reader of the English Bible. The word that means "total assurance" in Greek means "not so sure" in English. It is easy therefore to misunderstand many passages!

The true sense of the word "hope" is indicated in **verse 5** of Galatians 5, because Paul says that we simply "await" this righteousness. We don't work or strive for it. We know it is coming, on its way. So we can wait eagerly, rather than anxiously.

What is it that we await? Righteousness means more than goodness; it is a completely right record and right relationship with God. Paul is saying that we can live today in light of our certain, guaranteed, future **glorification** and welcome by God into His arms, because we know that "since you are a son, God has made you also an heir" (4:7). No one else, no **secular** person, no follower of any other religion, can look at their future like this! Non-religious people have no idea where they will be a million years from now, and religious people without the gospel are anxious about where they will be, and cannot relax or look forward to it with eagerness. The certainty of our future with God is a fruit of the gospel.

By referring to the future, Paul turns our imaginations to what it will mean to be radiant, glorious, beautiful and perfect. Elsewhere Paul says that Jesus lives to present us to Himself "radiant … without stain or wrinkle or any other blemish, but holy and blameless" (Ephesians 5:27). We know that this is guaranteed, and therefore, is essentially true now. We are to live today knowing we are, and always will be, an absolute beauty in the eyes of God. Put another way, we are as loved and honored by God now as we will be when we are perfectly radiant in heaven.

> We are to live knowing we are an absolute beauty in the eyes of God.

Paul says that through faith and by the work of the Spirit we can, and will, *eagerly* await this righteousness, this certain glory. So waiting is not simply an intellectual agreement about where we are headed. The language is too vivid and the results too powerful to be describing only that.

Paul is talking about a spiritual discipline. It is the development of an attitude of heart, an eager, passionate delight in all that we have been given in Christ. It involves meditation and reflection on our justification, adoption, and future glorification, and then bringing our actions into line with that. It is to ask:

We need to turn our minds to who we are and what we have in Christ so often that our hearts are stirred and our behavior brought into line with these unseen realities. This is something that happens in those who have faith in the Son, as the Spirit does His work.

Questions for reflection

1. Have you ever come close to losing (or actually lost) your gospel freedom? How did this happen? What lessons can you draw from it?

2. How much of a difference does your certain future hope make to your life now?

3. How can you make sure you meditate on your glorious future more often? What practical steps will you take?

PART TWO

Of no Value

We're used by now to Paul making breathtaking statements in his letter, and **verse 6** is another one: "Neither circumcision [representing religious duties] nor uncircumcision [representing paganism or immorality] has any value".

The word translated "value" means "to have power" when used to describe people, but when used of things it means "to be serviceable" or "to make a profit".

Neither moral exertion nor moral failure counts. Period.

Why? First, neither religion nor lack of religion count toward establishing a relationship with God. Paul has just said that our future acceptance with God is already certain through the work of Christ; we can eagerly and confidently await our glorious righteousness. In this context, when he says neither religion nor non-religion "count", he means they don't count toward our rightness and standing with God. Paul is saying: *My good performance does not make me right with God, nor does my bad performance really make me any more lost and hopeless. All stand equally lost and equally able to be saved.*

> Neither moral exertion nor moral failure counts. Period.

A Christian, when he or she has just experienced a success, should say: *But this success does not increase Christ's love for me. In fact, it is only because of His love for me that this happened, not the other way around!* And a Christian, when he or she has just experienced a failure, should say: *If I had not failed in this way, that would not make me any more loved and accepted by God than I am at this moment! My performance is irrelevant. In fact, God is always working for my good (Romans 8:28)—He has allowed this to happen because He loves me, not because He doesn't.* What a radical principle!

This should lead to tremendous peace and balance in a Christian life; it should eliminate huge ups and downs. For we are all in "circumcision" (spiritual success) or "uncircumcision" (spiritual failure) all the time, and Paul says that neither condition "counts".

Second, neither religion nor lack of religion count toward inner character change and a heart of real love. Circumcision and non-circumcision are "of no value" because "the only thing that counts is faith expressing itself through love" (**v 6**). Faith literally energizes love. And neither religious moralism nor **licentious** non-religiosity can do this, because both are essentially selfish and insecure. Selfishness and insecurity cannot produce love, because love is joyful self-giving. But faith in Christ can, because by it we are certain of our righteousness and welcome with the Father.

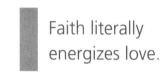

Faith literally energizes love.

Imagine what you would feel if a person asked to marry you, but you came to realize that they would not want you if you did not come with an inheritance. You would feel used. You would not feel loved at all. Now we all know that we don't feel loved by someone unless we are loved for who we are, not for what we bring him or her. This analogy helps us to understand the motivation of the gospel. When we thought our works saved us, we were serving God for what we could get from Him. We were using Him. But after the hope of the gospel settles in, and we see the grace and beauty of God, we love Him for who He is.

In the gospel, we see that Christ has died for us and valued us not for what we bring Him. We are of no profit to Him! We have been loved for our own sakes. And to the degree we see that in gospel faith, we respond in kind. Now we can serve God not for what He brings us, for we already have everything guaranteed, but for who He is and what He has done for us. Finally, we can love God for who He is. Also, now we can serve others not for what they bring us, but for who they are in themselves.

Increasingly, as **verse 5** dawns more and more on us, we live out **verse 6**. The more joy we have in our gracious salvation, the more we are driven by love and gratitude to do good for the sheer beauty of good, for sheer delight in God, for the sheer love of others. If we are reminding ourselves and living in light of our certain hope, we will have a heart overflowing with love. We don't need to seek righteousness and welcome from others, since these things are already ours; we are free to love others, seeking their good.

It is worth turning this around. Since our faith in Christ gives us certain hope, which overflows as love for others, if we find our love running dry or cold, the root of our lack of love is that we are not, by faith, looking at our hope. If we find ourselves unloving, the solution is not to seek to love better or more; it is to look at Christ, who gives us an unlosable, unshakable acceptance from the Father, and as we dwell on our hope, we will find our hearts melted by His love, and overflowing with His love to others.

So gospel freedom has at least two facets. There is "conscience freedom": I am free from the guilt of my imperfect performance. And there is "motivational freedom": I am free from the old drive to perform. I no longer need or want to follow the old pursuits as ways to win my righteousness or assure myself of worth.

Finish the Race

Paul interrupts his flow to warn the Galatian Christians once more. They had been "running a good race"—but now, as they listen to false teachers, they are being "kept ... from obeying the truth" (**v 7**). This is a great reminder that these are live issues, with eternal significance—there is a "penalty" to be paid (**v 10**).

What is particularly dangerous is that "the one who is throwing you into confusion" seems to have suggested that Paul probably agrees with him—that Paul is still (just as he did when he was a zealous Jew seeking salvation-through-obedience) "preaching circumcision" (**v 11**). He counters this by pointing out that God, "the one who calls you" (**v 8**), would never seek to persuade His people not to obey the truth of the gospel of the cross of Christ. There is, as we have continually seen, no compromise here; it is circumcision (self-salvation) or the "offense of the cross" (Christ-salvation—**v 11**). Paul is clearly preaching the latter, since he's being persecuted by those who want to trust in their own performance, just as all true gospel ministers will be (4:29).

We must not miss the urgency of Paul's words here, nor the anger he feels at those who have "cut in on you" (**v 7**). He wishes the false teachers, who are so forceful in pushing circumcision on believers, would go the whole way and castrate or "emasculate" themselves (**v 12**). As John Stott argues, this is a wish born not of a thirst for revenge, but deep love for the people of God:

> "I venture to say that if we were as concerned for God's church and God's word as Paul was, we too would wish that false teachers might cease from the land."
>
> (*The Message of Galatians*, page 136)

Paul's sentiment reminds us that this *matters*.

Don't Lose, Don't Abuse

After this emotionally charged diversion, Paul picks up his thread from verse 6. While the message of verses 1-12 is: *Don't **lose** gospel freedom*, **verses 13-15** warn us: *Don't **abuse** gospel freedom*.

We have seen throughout Galatians that it is extremely easy to lose our freedom by slipping back into legalism and works-righteousness. That is really the whole point of Paul's letter. Though Christians may profess intellectually a belief in the gospel, they do not always live in a way that is based on the gospel.

But now, Paul addresses the other main error that Christians can fall into—not legalism, but **license**. To fall back into rule-keeping means we lose our freedom, but to fall into **permissiveness** means we abuse our freedom. We have seen that gospel freedom is freedom that both takes away the guilt of sin and eats away at the motivation to sin. But Paul knows that such language as "freedom" can be very misleading to people. He knows that when he speaks of being "free from the law," some immediately think he means that people are now free to determine their own standards of behavior.

So he says in no uncertain terms that the gospel does not free you to sin! "Do not use your freedom to indulge the sinful nature" (**v 13**). Paul is continuing a thought that began back in **verse 7**: "You were running a good race. Who cut in on you and kept you from obeying the truth?" Christians do have to obey the truth, and there is a gospel dynamic or gospel motivation for obeying the truth that the Galatians used to have ("were running"), but which is now diminishing.

The gospel tells us that God is so holy that nothing short of complete payment for sins and the perfect righteousness of Christ can satisfy Him. On the other hand, the gospel tells us that God is so loving that we can receive this perfect righteousness now and stand complete in God's sight.

The gospel therefore neither leads us to live a guilty life (since God has lovingly accepted us), nor an unholy life (since the God who has accepted us is perfectly holy). To forget the first is to fall into the mistake Paul deals with in verse 1, and lose our freedom; to forget the second is to make the **verse 13** error, and abuse our freedom. Both mean we lose grasp of the gospel.

Squaring the Circle

This helps us to square the apparent circle in this passage. In **verse 3**, Paul implicitly says that Christians are freed from obligation to obey the whole law. Then in **verse 13**, he tells us to "serve one another in love"; and in **verse 14** he says that the summary of the law is to love one another! So Paul says bluntly that the Galatian Christians must obey the law. How do we understand this? Are we obliged, or are we not obliged?! Essentially, the answer is "yes". In one way we are obliged to keep the law, but in another way we are not.

If we look at **verse 3**, Paul immediately follows: "[You are] required to obey the whole law" with: "You … are trying to be justified by law" (**v 4**). The obligation that is gone for the Christian is the obligation to obey the law to be saved, which is impossible to achieve.

But now that we are saved wholly and freely by grace we are, if anything, *more* obligated to obey the law! Why? Because we have more reason to love God than we ever did before. Love arises from gospel faith and hope (**v 5-6**), and overflows into loving and serving our neighbors, rather than using them to serve ourselves. And loving our neighbor is "the entire law … summed up in a single command" (**v 14**).

> We have more reason to love God than we ever did before.

So Christians are freed from the law as a way to win merit from God, but we are *not* freed from the law as a way to please God. Rather, that obligation is increased. For the law is an expression of God's nature and heart, and thus we now doubly owe it to Him to use it to please and imitate Him. We owe it to Him as our Creator, since He designed us and owns us, and so He has both the wisdom to know how we are to live and the right to demand that we live that way. On the other hand, we now also owe it to Him as our Redeemer, since we gratefully want to please the one who saved us at such immeasurable cost.

Paul says that if you know God's love for you in Christ, if you know God's wisdom to you shown most clearly in Christ, why would you use your freedom to "indulge the sinful nature" (**v 13**), which left you an enemy of His, unforgiven and unfulfilled? The gospel devours the very motivation you have for sin. It completely saps your very need and reason to live any way you want. Anyone who insists that the gospel encourages us to sin has simply not understood it yet, nor begun to feel its power.

Take a lie, for example. On the one hand, gospel freedom means that I do not have to fear that I will be cast off from God if I lie. I am free from the legal penalty of that lie. The person who is seeking to be perfectly honest as a way of winning God's favor will be devastated when they slip and lie. But the gospel assures us that dishonesty will not condemn us.

However, let's ask: **Why** did I even **want** to lie? It will be because we felt that we needed what we faced losing if we told the truth. A person who must have approval, power, comfort or success to have joy or worth will lie to get, or to keep, that functional savior. A person who knows the gospel, in their affections as well as their intellectual understanding, will say: *I don't need this thing. Therefore I can tell the truth. If I lied, it would not change my standing before God—I'm free to lie. But there's no need to lie—why would I want to?*

The gospel does free you to live any way you want. But if you truly understand through the gospel who Jesus is and what He has done for you, then you will ask: *How can I live for Him?* And the answer will be—look at the will of God expressed in the law. The gospel frees

> The gospel frees us from the law, for the law.

us from the law, for the law. It does away with our old, selfishly motivated and unloving law-obedience. And it motivates us to obey the law out of love.

Questions for reflection

1. Do you react to your successes and failures in a gospel way, or a works-righteousness-based way?

2. In what situations do you find it hard to love others? How will remembering your hope increase your love?

3. Choose a sin you are struggling with. Why do you want to sin in this way? How does your gospel freedom undermine that motivation to sin?

11. GOSPEL CHARACTER

In normal religion, the motivation for morality is fear-based. In gospel Christianity, the motivation is a dynamic of love, as we saw in the last chapter (5:6, 14). And now, Paul spells out just *how* we grow in character through this new dynamic. And his headline is: *We grow as we battle.*

The Struggle

There are two natures at work in every Christian: the Spirit and the sinful nature (**v 16**). And at any point in our life, we will "live by" one, and "not gratify" the other. Paul, of course, encourages the Galatians to "live by the Spirit".

The "sinful nature" translates the Greek word *sarx,* which in some Bible versions is rendered "flesh". The flesh in the New Testament, when opposed to the Spirit, does not refer to our physical nature as opposed to our spiritual nature, but to the sin-desiring aspect of our whole being as opposed to the God-desiring aspect. The *sarx* is our sinful heart. Or rather, it is the part or the aspect of our hearts which is not yet renewed by the Spirit.

Set against, or "contrary to" (**v 17**), the sinful nature is the Spirit. At first sight, it may seem that this is a battle between something inside us (our *sarx*) and outside us (the Holy Spirit). But since Paul talks of each side as producing character qualities within us, and because of his language of two kinds of "desires", it is clear that this conflict takes place within us. It's most accurate to think of "the Spirit" as the renewed Christian heart, made new by the Holy Spirit. Our sinful nature was there, ruling alone and unopposed, before we were Christians. The Spirit, however, entered **supernaturally** when we first became Christians and has begun a renewal that is now our "new nature". So in Ephesians 4:22-24, Paul refers to this *sarx* versus Spirit conflict as the competition between "the old self" (or "man") and "the new self" (or "man").

What precisely is the nature of the "conflict" (**v 17**)? It is a battle between the "desires" of the Spirit and the *sarx*. Literally, Paul calls the "desires of the sinful nature" *epithumia*. In the older versions, this word was translated "lust", which led the reader to think of sexual desire. In modern translations the word is just translated "desires"; but that is maybe even more unhelpful.

Literally, *epithumia* means an "over-desire", an "inordinate desire"; an all-controlling drive and longing. This is crucial. The main problem our heart has is not so much desires for bad things, but our over-desires for good things. When a good thing becomes our "god", it creates "over-desires" (see Ephesians 2:3; 1 Peter 2:11; 1 John 2:16). Paul says that sinful desires become deep things that drive and control us. Sin creates in us the feeling that we must have this, or that, or the other.

> The main problem is not our desires for bad things, but our over-desires for good things.

David Powlison has a very helpful insight on this:

"If 'idolatry' is the characteristic and summary Old Testament word for our drift from God, then 'desires' (epithumia) is the characteristic and summary New Testament word for that same drift ... The New Testament merges the concept of idolatry and the concept of inordinate, life-ruling desires ... for lust, craving, yearning and greedy demand (Ephesians 5:5; Colossians 3:5)."

(*The Journal of Biblical Counseling*, page 36)

One of the most intriguing statements here is when Paul literally says in **verse 17**: "The flesh over-desires against the Spirit, and the Spirit against the flesh". Notice that Paul does not actually say that the Spirit "over-desires" (how could the Spirit desire something too much?), yet the construction indicates that the Spirit has passions and yearnings as well, and that they are at least as strong! What is it that the Spirit longs for? Jesus teaches that the Holy Spirit will come into the world to "glorify me" (John 16:14, ESV). So, while our flesh glorifies and adores and yearns for all kinds of created things and conditions and people, the Spirit glorifies and adores and yearns for Jesus. The Spirit speaks of the beauty and greatness of Christ.

The Spirit, then, longs to show us Christ and to **conform** us to Christ. And ultimately, this is what the Christian wants, too. It is easy to overlook, but Paul makes an extremely telling statement when he says the Spirit and the *sarx* "are in conflict with each other so that you do not do what you want" (**Galatians 5:17**). This is a parallel passage to Romans 7:22-23, where he says that "in my inner being I delight in God's law", yet he finds there is "another law at work in the members of my body, waging war against the law of my mind".

> The Spirit longs to conform us to Christ. Ultimately, this is what the Christian wants, too.

Living the way of the Spirit is what we most deeply "want", yet the sinful nature continues to generate alternative and competing desires which we experience and can give in to, but which now contradict our most abiding love and goals. The **reborn** person has both sinful desires and godly desires, but "we" most truly want what our Spirit-renewed heart wants.

This statement is filled with hope and affirmation. Even when we are falling into sin, we can say, with Paul: *This is not the real me; this is not what I really want. I want God and His will.*

How the *Sarx* Works

There is a striking **parallelism** between **verse 16** and **verse 18**. We are to "live by the Spirit … [be] led by the Spirit", in contrast to choosing to "gratify … the sinful nature" or be "under law".

For Paul, these two things are either very closely linked, or even just different ways of speaking about the same thing. This tells us not just something about the actions of the sinful nature, but also about the motives of the sinful nature; not just that it disobeys God, but why it "wants" to.

The sinful nature is that within us which wants us to be our own savior and lord. The *sarx*-heart functions "under law"; it rejects the free gift of Christ's righteousness and salvation, and continues to seek its own. Therefore, the sin underneath all sins—the motive for our disobedience—is always a lack of trust in God's grace and goodness, and a desire to protect and guard our own lives through self-salvation.

In light of this, we can see that the two natures Paul speaks of are really two semi-intact motivational systems within us. A motivational system is centered on a goal that the imagination finds beautiful and desirable. This goal generates what we perceive as "needs", and manufactures "drives" to attain them. The sinful nature is really our old motivational system—with its own goals and thus its own needs and drives—still somewhat intact. It is focusing on some object that is in itself good, but which it turns into an idol by which we seek our salvation ("I can have worth if I am loved… if I have a good career… if my children love me"), and which finally then creates over-desire for that idol.

What the *Sarx* Works

Verses 19-21 list "the acts of the sinful nature" (**v 19**). Notice they are not all actions; attitudes are just as much over-desires of our *sarx*.

There are three words in **verse 19** having to do with the works of the flesh in the area of sexuality: sexual immorality (*porneia*), which is sexual intercourse between unmarried people; impurity (*akatharsia*), ie: unnatural sexual practices and relationships; debauchery (*aselgia*), ie: uncontrolled sexuality.

There are two words in **verse 20** having to do with the area of religion: idolatry (*eidololatria*) and witchcraft (*pharmakeia*). Because idolatry is paired with witchcraft here, it is not referring to the very broad, inclusive practice of making good things like career into a "god" (as it is in Ephesians 5:5 and Colossians 3:5). Rather, Paul is referring to very specific occult and pagan religious practices. The first is providing an inadequate substitute for God, and the second is faking the work of the Spirit.

Then, in **verses 20-21,** come eight words that describe how the flesh destroys relationships. Four of these are destructive attitudes: selfish ambition (*eritheia*), namely competitiveness, a self-seeking motive; envy (*phthonoi*), coveting, desiring what others have; jealousy (*zdlos*), the zeal and energy that comes from a hungry ego; and hatred (*echthrai*), meaning hostility, an adversarial attitude. Four describe the

The flesh destroys relationships.

results of these attitudes in relationships: discord (*eris*), being argumentative or seeking to pick fights; fits of rage (*thumoi*), outbursts of anger; dissensions (*dichostaiai*), divisions between people (which is what rage leads to); and factions (*aireseis*), permanent parties and warring groups.

Finally, there are two words that refer to substance abuse: drunkenness and orgies. These two words are linked. Orgies are not "sex orgies" but "drinking orgies". One of the works of the flesh is addiction to pleasure-creating substances and behavior.

Paul has a stark warning for "those who live like this ... [they] will not inherit the kingdom of God" (**v 21**). Paul is referring to habitual practice, rather than infrequent, and repented-of, lapses. For someone continually to indulge the sinful nature without battling against it is to show that the Son has not redeemed them, and that the Spirit has not renewed them. Paul is not looking to undermine Christian assurance here; but he is aiming to banish complacency.

Another way to break down this list into categories is to notice that some of the sins are characteristic of religious people (selfishness, envy, jealousy, factions), while others are more characteristic of non-religious people (immorality, drunkenness). This list shows us that God does not make the kind of distinctions that we commonly do, seeing sex and drink as more sinful than jealousy and ambition. It undermines the tendency of naturally non-religious people to label the flaws of someone else's religious *sarx* as "worse", and of religious people to see the works of a non-religious *sarx* as beyond the pale. We are much better at noticing the works of someone else's sinful nature than we are at battling our own!

Questions for reflection

1. Which of the works of the sinful nature do you see in your life?

2. What are the over-desires that cause you to think or behave in these ways?

3. How will you preach the gospel of grace and acceptance to yourself to undermine these over-desires?

PART TWO

To be "led by the Spirit" (**v 18**) is to change, and be changed, to be the people we want to be. The Spirit-fuelled development of Christ-like character is liberating, because it brings us closer to being the people we were designed to be, the people our Spirit-renewed hearts want us to be.

Why Paul Said "Fruit"

Paul always chooses his images carefully. And it is very revealing that he talks about "acts" of the sinful nature (**v 19**), but then switches to speak of "the fruit of the Spirit" (**v 22**). The single word "fruit" takes us to the world of agriculture, and tells us four things about how the Spirit works.

First, Christian growth is ***gradual***—as gradual as a turnip or potato growing. With botanical growth, you never see it happening—you can only measure it after a time. With the growth of the fruit of the Spirit, it might be growing in a Christian's life, but they never realize until a trouble or difficulty shows up and they think: *A couple of years ago I would never have been so patient or self-controlled in this situation.* That shows that the fruit of the Spirit has been growing, gradually and unnoticed.

Second, the growth of the Spirit's fruit is ***inevitable***. There will be growth. There's a story about a man who, when he died, was buried under a marble slab, and somehow an acorn got into his grave. Over time, gradually and unnoticed, the acorn grew. And eventually, it split open the marble, such was its power. Marble, or a tiny seed? If you don't know about how things grow, you'd bet on the marble! But of course, in fact the money should be on the acorn.

If someone has the Spirit in them—if they are a Christian—the fruit will grow. Whatever a Christian's life is like, the fruit of the Spirit will burst through. It's inevitable. This is encouraging to us as we think of how marble-like our sinful nature is; but it is also challenging. It forces us to ask, if we've been Christians for a few years or more: *Is there fruit growing in my life?* We are saved by faith, not by growing fruit; but we are not saved by fruitless faith. A person saved by faith will be a person in whom the fruit of the Spirit grows.

> We are saved by faith; but we are not saved by fruitless faith.

Third, the fruit of the Spirit has **internal** roots. It is not about **traits** or characteristics. It is about a change much deeper than that. Think about an apple tree. Do the apples on the tree make it alive? No—if you tied apples onto a dead tree's branches, that wouldn't make it alive! The apples don't give life; they are a sign that the tree is alive. But the life produces the fruit; not the other way around.

We tend to see **gifts** as the sign of the Spirit's work in someone. But the Bible never does. Judas and King Saul were used by the Spirit to prophesy, do miracles, and so on… but they did not have Spirit-renewed hearts.

To be truly led by the Spirit is to grow "the fruit of the Spirit" (**v 22**). Gifts may or may not operate out of a grace-changed heart; but the fruit-growth of the Spirit can only happen in a child of God. The only test that the Spirit has really indwelled you as a child of God is the growth in the fruit of the Spirit. The first part of that fruit, which Paul mentions here is "love"; and as he says elsewhere, to a church which over-desired particular spiritual gifts: "If I speak in the tongues of men and of angels, but have not love, I am only a resounding gong … I am nothing … I gain nothing" (1 Corinthians 13:1, 2, 3).

Fourth, Christian growth is **symmetrical**. Paul deliberately uses the singular word "fruit" to describe a whole list of things that grow in a Spirit-filled person. From this we learn a very important point for understanding and discerning the fruit of the Spirit. The real fruit of the Spirit always grow up together. They are one. Jonathan Edwards put it like this: "There is a concatenation of the graces of Christianity". That is, you do not get one part of the fruit of the Spirit growing without all the parts growing.

When we look at the list of fruits, we notice that we are naturally stronger in some than in others. But our strengths, apart from the Holy Spirit, are due to natural temperament (we have a trait through brain chemistry and/or early training), or to natural self-interest (we learned a trait in order to handle some issue or condition we met). For example, some people are temperamentally gentle and diplomatic (gentleness). But the sign that this is not due to the work of the Holy Spirit is that such people are usually not bold or courageous (faithfulness). Because of what Paul says about the unity of the fruit, this means that this sort of gentleness is not real spiritual humility, but just temperamental sweetness.

John says: "If anyone says, 'I love God,' yet hates his brother, he is a liar" (1 John 4:20). Notice that he does not say: *If a man loves God but doesn't love his brother, he is unbalanced.* No, he says he is a liar. True love to God (love) is always accompanied by love to others (kindness). If they are not both there, neither are there at all.

There are many, many cases of this. Some folks seem happy and bubbly (joy) and are good at meeting new people, but are very unreliable and cannot keep friends (faithfulness). This is not real joy but just being an extrovert by nature. Some people seem very unflappable and unbothered (peaceful) but they are not kind or gentle. That is not real peace, but indifference and perhaps cynicism. It enables you to get through the difficulties of life without being always hurt, but it desensitizes you and makes you much less approachable.

The Parts of the Fruit

It is worth looking closely at each aspect of the singular fruit of the Spirit (**v 22-23**):

1. *Agape = love.* It means to serve a person for their good and intrinsic value, not for what the person brings you. Its opposite is fear:

self-protection and abusing people. Its counterfeit (a fake version) is selfish affection, where you are attracted to someone and treat them well because of how they make you feel about yourself.

2. *Chara = joy,* a delight in God for the sheer beauty and worth of who He is. Its opposite is hopelessness or despair, and its counterfeit is an elation that is based on experiencing blessings, not the Blesser, causing mood swings based on circumstances.

3. *Irene = peace,* meaning a confidence and rest in the wisdom and control of God, rather than in your own. It replaces anxiety and worry. The fake version of peace is indifference, apathy, not caring about something.

4. *Makrothumia = patience,* an ability to face trouble without blowing up or hitting out. Its opposite is resentment toward God and others, and its counterfeits are cynicism or lack of care: *This is too small to care about.*

5. *Chrestotes = kindness,* which is an ability to serve others practically in a way which makes me vulnerable, which comes from having a deep inner security. Its opposite is envy, which leaves me unable to rejoice in another's joy. And its fake alternative is manipulative good deeds, doing good for others so I can congratulate myself and feel I am "good enough" for others or for God.

6. *Agathosune = goodness, integrity;* being the same person in every situation, rather than a phony or a hypocrite. This is not the same as being always truthful but not always loving; getting things off your chest just to make yourself feel or look better.

7. *Pistis = faithfulness, loyalty, courage,* to be utterly reliable and true to your word. Its opposite is to be an opportunist, a friend only in good times. And its counterfeit is to be loving but not truthful, so that you are never willing to confront or challenge.

8. *Prautas = gentleness, humility, self-forgetfulness.* The opposite is to be superior or self-absorbed. Humility is not the same as inferiority (see next chapter).

9. *Egkrateia = self-control,* the ability to pursue the important over

the urgent, rather than to be always impulsive or uncontrolled. The slightly surprising counterfeit is a willpower which is based on pride, the need to feel in control.

When we look closely at the fruit of the Spirit, and see that one aspect of it cannot be seen in isolation from any of the others, we see that we are far more in need of growth in the fruit of the Spirit than we think. When we stop looking at our gifts as a sign that we are Christlike, and stop looking at our natural strengths as a sign we are Christlike, but challenge ourselves to look at the nature, unity and definitions of the Spirit, we have a much deeper sense of how we lack these things.

Growing the Fruit of the Spirit

How, then, can the fruit of the Spirit take root in our hearts and be produced in our lives? Paul immediately supplies the answer.

First, we need to remember that we "belong to Christ Jesus" (**v 24**). All that is His, is ours. Our approval and welcome from the Father rests not on our character or actions, but on His. We are free to acknowledge where we have given up ground to the *sarx* in our lives; free to confess where we have not sought to keep in step with the Spirit; free to realize where we have confused our gifts or natural character with the fruit of the Spirit.

Second, because we belong to Christ we "have crucified the sinful nature with its passions and desires" (literally "over-desires", **v 24**). "Crucifying the sinful nature" is really the identification and disman- tling of idols. It means to put an end to the ruling and attractive power that idols have in our lives, and so to destroy their ability to agitate and inflame our thoughts and desires. Crucifying the *sarx* is about stran- gling sin at the motivational level, rather than simply setting ourselves against sin at the behavioral level. Real changes in our lives cannot proceed without us discerning our particular "characteristic flesh"— the idols and desires that come from our individual sinful nature.

> We have to ask ourselves not just *what* we do wrong, but *why* we do it wrong.

We have to ask ourselves not just *what* we do wrong, but *why* we do it wrong. We disobey God in order to get something we feel we *must* have. That's an "over-desire". Why must we have it? Because it is a way we are trying to keep "under law". It is something we have come to believe will *authenticate* us. To crucify the sinful nature is to say: *Lord, my heart thinks that I must have this thing, otherwise I have no value. It is a pseudo-savior. But to think and feel and live like this is to forget what I mean to you, how you see me in Christ. By your Spirit, I will reflect on your love for me in Him until this thing loses its attractive power over my soul.*

It is worth briefly noticing what crucifying the sinful nature does not mean. Paul is not saying: *Be hard on yourself, especially the body.* For example, it is an old tradition to give up something for Lent. Usually this means to refuse to satisfy some needs for rest, comfort, or pleasure. This is a serious mistake. It is obvious from the list of the acts of the sinful nature (**v 19-21**) that many of them have nothing to do with the body (eg: ambition, jealousy, envy). Asceticism—the denial of pleasure—does not touch these.

Next, Paul is not simply saying: *Just say "no" to sin.* Our *sarx* desires to live under the law in some way. It instinctively wants to find a form of self-salvation. Just to say no without examining the motives underneath wrong behavior can actually be part of a new form of seeking self-righteousness, as we seek to justify ourselves by saying no to ungodly attitudes and actions. The Galatians were on the verge of "just saying no" to a lot of things, but in a way which Paul was warning would leave them "alienated from Christ" (v 4).

Last, Paul is not talking of a **passive process**. A Christian can say "I have been crucified with Christ" (2:20), as something that has been done to us; we are as free from the condemnation of sin as if we had already paid the penalty ourselves with our own death. Christ's death was our death. But **5:24** is talking about an ongoing "crucifixion" which we ourselves do to our sinful nature, as we put to death the old nature within us.

So third, we need to "keep in step with the Spirit" (**v 25**). This is a positive process (not simply giving things up), an active process (which we do), and something more than simple obedience (though it is not less than simple obedience). The Spirit is a living person, who glories in and magnifies the work of Jesus. Once we specifically find the particular false beliefs of our flesh which generate the "over-desires" and lead us to sin, we must replace them with Christ.

This is not just an intellectual exercise. We must worship Christ, with the help of the Holy Spirit, adoring Him until our hearts find Him more beautiful than the object we felt we had to have. As we do that, we will put to death our old *sarx* nature, clearing room for the fruit of the Spirit to grow; and we will find that fruit growing, changing us more and more into the people we long to be, and God desires us to be.

Questions for reflection

1. Examine yourself. How can you see the fruit of the Spirit growing in your life?

2. Do you have natural characteristics which could be confused with the fruit of the Spirit?

3. What are the idols which need identifying and dismantling in your life? How can you replace them with Christ?

12. GOSPEL RELATIONSHIPS

What difference does the gospel make to your relationships? How does it affect the way you look at yourself in terms of those around you; and how you look at others in terms of yourself?

This is a very short passage, but it is bristling with practical principles for relating to others. The gospel creates a whole new self-image which is not based on comparisons with others. Only the gospel makes us neither self-confident nor self-disdaining, but both bold and humble. That works itself out in relationships with everyone. Rather than comparing ourselves with those "above" or "below", we look only at our own responsibility to take what we have and are, and offer it to God as a sacrifice of gratitude for what Christ has done.

Honor-Hunger

Paul has just encouraged his fellow Christians to "keep in step with the Spirit" (5:25). As we saw in the last chapter, this involves an internal, daily crucifixion of our sinful over-desires, and a daily heart-adoration of Christ, so that the fruit of the Spirit will grow in our character.

Now Paul wants to show how keeping in step with the Spirit will transform our relationships. And at its heart, it will mean that we do "not become [or, in some cases, stop being!] conceited" (**v 26**).

The Greek word translated "conceit" here is *kenodoxoi,* which literally means "vain-glorious" or "empty of honor". So conceit is a deep insecurity, a perceived absence of honor and glory, leading to a need to prove our worth to ourselves and others. This in turn fixates our mind on comparing ourselves with others. When we seem better than someone else in some trait, our "honor-hunger" puffs us up and makes us feel great. When we seem to be inferior to someone else, we are devastated for the same reason. In addition, "honor-hunger" can make us very competitive. This describes the natural state of our heart without the gospel.

If we are conceited, we will be "provoking and envying each other" (**v 26**). "Provoke"—*prokaleo*—is competitive, meaning to challenge someone to a contest. "Envy" means to want something that rightfully belongs to someone else, or to want that person not to have that thing.

It is possible that Paul is simply describing people who are hostile (provoking) to people that they envy. But more likely (as John Stott believes), Paul is talking of two different ways of relating to others. "Provoking" is the stance of someone who is sure of his or her superiority, looking down on someone perceived to be weaker. "Envying" is the stance of someone who is conscious of inferiority, looking "up" at someone they feel is above them.

So Paul is saying that both superiority *and* inferiority are a form of conceit. This is striking, and profound. Both the superior and the inferior person are self-absorbed. In both cases, you are focusing heavily on how the other person makes you look and feel instead of how you make him or her look and feel.

> Both the superior and the inferior person are self-absorbed.

Another way to put it is in terms of works-righteousness, which joins **verse 26** to the underlying theme of the letter: the need for us to live in line with the gospel, and not retreat back into living by works. Both the "superior" and the "inferior" person are trying to gain worth through competition, at the expense of others. Both want to gain an identity by beating and surpassing others. Both want to be proud and superior.

The only difference between the person of arrogance and the person with low self-esteem is that the inferior person has lost at the game, and despairs about themselves and envies those they see as "winners". The superior person, on the other hand, feels as though they have, for the moment, won, and continually compares themselves with others to check they are still winning. Of course, much of the time we are both provoking in one area of our lives and envying in another.

So though provoking and envying seem like exact opposites, they are both forms of conceit. As C.S. Lewis pointed out, humility is not thinking less of yourself: it is thinking of yourself less. Self-flagellation and low self-esteem are not marks of gospel humility. They are just as much a rejection of the gospel as are pride and self-confidence!

So both the superiority complex and the inferiority complex are, at root, born of insecurity and inferiority. They are just two different outworkings of our desire to gain glory for ourselves, to feel worthwhile as people. **Verse 26** is essentially saying: *Do not let your hunger for honor make you either despise or envy people.*

Provocative or Envious?

While we may well be a mixture of the two, most of us naturally tend toward either provoking or envying as the outworkings of our conceit. How can I analyze which I am? By asking:

- Do I have a tendency to "blow up" or do I tend to "clam up?"

- Do I tend to pick arguments with people or do I completely avoid confrontation?

- Do I tend to get very down on individuals and groups of people or am I more often embarrassed and intimidated around certain classes or kinds of people?

- When criticized, do I get very angry and very judgmental—and simply attack right back? Or do I get very discouraged and very defensive—make lots of excuses, or give right in?

■ Do I often think: *I would never, ever do what this person has done?* or do I often look at people and say: *I could never, ever accomplish what this person does?*

A Gospel-based Self-image

The Spirit works in us to apply the gospel to our self-perception and view of others. He creates a whole new self-image which is not based on comparisons with others.

Only the gospel makes us neither self-confident nor self-disdaining, but both bold and humble. That works itself out in relationships with everyone. The gospel is the only thing that addresses conceit, the vain-glory. To the degree I am still functionally earning my worth through performance (ie: still functioning in works-righteousness), to that degree I will be either operating out of superiority or inferiority. Why? Because if I am saved by my works, then I can either be confident but not humble (superior, provoking, because I feel I'm "winning") or humble but not confident (inferior and envious, because I feel I'm losing). Apart from the gospel, I will be forced to be superior or inferior, or to swing back and forth, or to be one way with some people and another way with others. I am continually caught between these two ways, because of the nature of my self-image.

But the gospel creates a new self-image, as we have seen previously. It *humbles* me before anyone, telling me I am a sinner saved only by grace. But it also **emboldens** me before anyone, telling me I am loved and honored by the only eyes in the universe that really count.

So the gospel gives me a boldness and a humility that can co-exist, and that can increase together.

> The gospel gives me a boldness and a humility that can co-exist.

Practically speaking, you have to use the gospel by preaching it to yourself right in the midst of the situations where you are trying to act in newness of life. If, for example, you find yourself being very defensive around someone, you must use the gospel at that very moment, saying to yourself: *What **you** think of me is not the important thing. Jesus Christ's approval of me, not yours, is my righteousness, my identity, my worth.* If, on the other hand, you find yourself looking down on someone, you need to remind yourself of the gospel: *What **I** think of me is not the important thing. I am just as much a sinner, and just as undeserving of Christ's love for me, as this person.*

When we feel conceited—superior *or* inferior—we need to root our glory, our sense of worth, in who we are in and through Christ. We need to think to ourselves, and ask the Spirit to help us apply to our emotions, the truth of 3:26, that: *I am a son of God—I can be confident—through faith in Christ Jesus—I am humble.*

Conceit in Relationships

In chapter 5, Paul has laid out two errors, both of which oppose the gospel: losing freedom by seeking salvation through keeping rules (moralism), and abusing freedom by rejecting the idea of rules at all (hedonism).

When it comes to relationships, the moralist's conceit shows itself in their need of others' approval, or their need of other's reliance on them. They need others' approval or reliance to show that they are doing well enough. But this means their role in relationships is essentially selfish—others exist to validate them, to prove their righteousness.

The hedonist's conceit, on the other hand, shows itself in their lack of commitment. They need others only for the pleasure or satisfaction they offer them; as soon as a relationship entails major sacrifice, the hedonist bails out. Their relationships are self-serving.

So, for example, when it comes to relating to parents, moralism will either make you so concerned to please your parents that you can't live without continually thinking of them, or so mad at them for their control or neglect of your life that you also cannot live without thinking of them. Hedonism means you don't relate to them at all, except when it suits you.

The gospel frees us from the moralist's need to find salvation in pleasing or rejecting our parents; it tells us we have a perfect Father. And it challenges the hedonist's refusal to think of their parents at all, because we are obligated to love others.

Or take sexual relationships as another example. The moralist tends to see sex as dirty or at least a dangerous impulse that leads constantly to sin. The uneasy conscience of the moralist will lead to either complete avoidance or to a very driven, breathless need for sexual experience. Both come from a glory-vacuum within, which can make sex into a way to fill the emptiness.

> A glory-vacuum within can make sex into a way to fill the emptiness.

On the other hand, the hedonist sees sex as merely a biological and physical appetite. They will likely be less **convoluted** and troubled about sex, yet they have also given up on the deep longing of their heart to have union with someone sexually who is completely, unconditionally, and permanently true to them. So deep fulfillment will always be elusive.

But the gospel shows us that sex is part of God's good creation. And sexuality is to reflect the self-giving of Christ. He gave Himself completely. So we are not to seek intimacy sexually but then hold back control of our lives. If we give ourselves sexually, we are to give ourselves legally, socially, personally—utterly. Sex is only to happen in a totally committed, permanent relationship of marriage. Through Christ's transformation of us, that ideal is somewhat realizable even though our marriages always contain two sinners.

Questions for reflection

1. Using the questions on pages 161-162, do you tend to be provocative or envious?

2. How does your conceit show itself in your relationships?

3. How will having a self-image based on the gospel change the way you see yourself and see others? When do you particularly need to preach the gospel to yourself?

PART TWO

Helping our Brothers

To "become conceited"—to seek our own glory in relationships—means that, however close we are to someone else, our treatment of them must always be tinged with selfishness. The gospel undermines that—it enables us to live as "brothers" (**6:1**).

And brothers (and sisters) are able to encourage one another in their Christian lives. "If someone is caught in a sin" (**v 1**), conceited superiority would drive us to look down on them, be glad we are not like them, and feel righteous in ourselves. Pointing out their sin would merely be to underline how good we look by comparison. Conceited inferiority would cause us either to envy the life they are leading, however sinful; or to crave their approval so much that we won't risk pointing out their failure to live in line with the gospel.

What will a "brother", who knows they are a son of God, do? Paul says we will not ignore a situation when we see someone "caught" in a sin. This does not mean that we are to confront anyone we see sinning in any way. "Love covers over a multitude of sins" (1 Peter 4:8)—we are not to be quick to criticize and tell people about their faults (see also 1 Corinthians 13:5, 7). But we must not overlook someone "caught"—overtaken—by a sin. This indicates that the sinful behavior is a pattern, and a particular sin has, in a sense, gotten the upper hand with this person. It is a habit of sinful behavior that the person will not be able to overcome without help and outside intervention. Christians need to be neither quick to criticize nor afraid to confront.

> We need to be neither quick to criticize, nor afraid to confront.

We will accept our responsibility, as Spirit-filled brothers, to help. Paul is speaking to "you who are spiritual" (**v 1**); that is, to those who "live by the Spirit" (5:16, 25). He is not referring to some super-spiritual group of elite Christians; he is saying to ordinary Christians: *If you follow the desires of the Spirit, you will do this.* This responsibility belongs to anyone who is trying to live a Christian life at all.

What will our aim be? To "restore him gently" (**v 1**). The Greek translated "restore" here is *katartizdo*. This was the term used for setting a dislocated bone back into place. A dislocated bone is extremely painful, because it is not in its designed, natural relationship to the other parts of the body. To put a bone back in place will inevitably inflict pain, but it is a healing pain. It means we are to confront, even when that will be painful, but our confronting must be aiming to prompt a change of life and heart.

But a "brother" will confront "gently". Paul says this gentleness will only come if you "watch yourself, or you also may be tempted" (**v 1**). This is difficult, but practical, advice. We won't be able to winsomely confront someone if we think we are not capable of similar or equal sin. If we do feel we are above the person, our air of superiority will come through and we will destroy, not restore.

Carry each other's Burdens

Confronting someone caught in a sin is a way to "carry each other's burdens" (**v 2**), though, of course, not the only way. In verse 2 Paul is bringing together the other-centered approach—which replaces conceit as the Spirit roots our sense of worth in Christ—and the gospel-motivated obedience of the law which he outlined in chapter 5. "Brothers ... who are spiritual" (**6:1**) will "carry each other's burdens, and in this way ... will fulfill the law of Christ" (**v 2**).

Verse 2, then, reflects 5:13-14: "Serve one another in love ... The entire law is summed up in a single command: 'Love your neighbor as yourself'." The law of Christ is the law which is summed up as love-your-neighbor. Why would the law of neighbor-love be called the law of Christ? Because Christ is the ultimate and unsurpassable example of this kind of love. We are to love others as Christ loved us (John 13:34; Ephesians 4:32). Though the whole Old Testament law could be summed up in the command to love, it is Christ's life and death that becomes the supreme embodiment of what this love should be. When we look at His life and attitude and all His dealings, we have, in a sense, "a law", a breathtaking model of the kind of life we should live.

Placing **6:2** and 5:13-14 alongside each other shows us that to "serve one another in love" means to "carry each other's burdens". This brings the lofty concept of love down to earth. We are not to let people carry their burdens alone. These "burdens" can be a simple responsibility, like raising a child or renovating a living space. Or they can be a difficulty, a problem. By characterizing the responsibilities and problems of life as "burdens", Paul very vividly and practically teaches how a Christian relates to others. You cannot help with a burden unless you come very close to the burdened person, standing virtually in their shoes, and putting your own strength under the burden so its weight is distributed on both of you, lightening the load of the other. So in the same way, a Christian must listen and understand, and physically, emotionally, spiritually, take up some of the burden with the other person.

> You cannot help with a burden unless you come very close to the burdened person.

It is probable that Paul is taking one more swipe at the "Judaizers", the false teachers who were trying to get the Galatians to come under the law of Moses. These requirements had been described as a "yoke", a burden, by the Council of Jerusalem, which met to decide the controversy over Gentile Christians' obligations to obey the Jewish ceremonial law (Acts 15:10). Paul is telling the Galatians that, rather than placing themselves under the burden of law-fulfillment, they should be lifting burdens off others—and that, ultimately, this is the way to fulfill the law!

"Law of Christ" means modeling our whole life on the example of Christ, motivated by grateful joy. It is a life centered on a person rather than a code. We have a different kind of obligation upon us than we did before. Now we bear others' burdens because Christ bore ours. **Verse 2** could be summed up as: *Bear others' burdens, and by doing this follow in the footsteps of Christ, who bore yours.*

Carry your own Load

We will not be able to bear each other's burdens, though, unless we have a proper, gospel-based self-view. **Verses 3-5** are, essentially, an intriguing discussion of humility and pride. The NIV translation doesn't reflect it, but **verse 3** begins "for"; that is, if you make the mistake outlined in verse 3, you won't be able to do the burden-bearing of verse 2.

So, if "anyone thinks he is something when he is nothing" (**v 3**), they will be too self-important to have a servant heart, to look around and notice the burdens of others and help them with them. This is a stern warning, and we should not **relativize** Paul's statement that we are "nothing". Of course, a Christian is filled with hope and confidence, but it is because of Christ. As Jesus Himself said: "Apart from me, you can do nothing" (John 15:5). It takes Christ-centered humility to bear the burdens of others.

Nevertheless, there is a legitimate "pride in himself" which a Christian can have (**v 4**). This is totally different from the conceited pride of superiority or inferiority, which makes us and our glory the ground of our motivations and actions. Conceit leads to the Christian "comparing himself to someone else" (**v 4**) in a bid to feel proud, or worthwhile. On the one hand, we may not truly be very loving, but if we are surrounded by selfish people, we will have great pride in our relative love, and not seek to grow in love. On the other, we may be living up to our God-given capacities, but since we are surrounded by very gifted people, we will be greatly discouraged and not appreciate what God has made us and given us.

Instead, we should "test" our "own actions" (**v 4**). This means we are to assess our own opportunities (gifts and tests as God has afforded them) and our own responses to them. We should measure ourselves, in a sense, against ourselves.

Connecting **verse 5** to **verse 4** helps explain an apparent contradiction in this section. How can we possibly "carry each other's burdens" (**v 2**) when "each should carry his own load" (**v 5**)?! Because load is not the same as burdens. The Greek word translated "burdens" means a heavy weight, but the different Greek word translated "load" refers to a kind of backpack. **Verse 5** means that God has given each of us a different set of difficulties and opportunities, a different set of weaknesses and gifts. These are our "load"—our responsibility before God.

We are therefore not to compare ourselves with others. Instead, we must look at our particular tests and duties and respond to them obediently. If we see life in this way, we will judge our life each day against who we have been, and who we could have been. When we see progress, we will take legitimate pride in it, whether or not we are better or worse than someone else. We will not compare ourselves with someone who has done less than us (and feel conceited pride) or someone who has done more (and feel conceited despair or envy). God has given them a different load to carry and to serve Him with. Our task is to carry *our* individual load, not someone else's, in a way that pleases God.

> Our task is to carry our individual load in a way that pleases God.

If we see life this way, we will be slow to judge others as well. We will be non-judgmental and generous. For example, if we see someone being irritable, we will think: *I don't know what pressures that person is facing, nor what level of emotional self-control he began with. Maybe he is actually obeying God better than me today!*

We are humbly and gently to help others with their tasks and problems, with all their burdens. But:

"There is one burden that we cannot share ... and that is our responsibility to God on the day of judgment. On that day you cannot carry my pack and I cannot carry yours."

(John Stott, *The Message of Galatians*, page 160)

Questions for reflection

1. Is there a habitual sin you need to gently restore a brother from? Are you willing to listen to others who seek to restore you?

2. What opportunities has God given you to carry another's burdens?

3. How is it liberating to know that you will only answer for your own load, and not how you lived compared to others?

13. SOWING AND REAPING

These final words of Paul's may at first sight seem like a series of disconnected statements, but Paul is actually doing two things as he signs off. Verses 6-10 are his final warning; and verses 11-18 are his final invitation. His warning and his invitation are essentially the same message, the message that underlies every line of this letter: live by the gospel!

The Teacher and the Taught

Paul's first instruction in this section both looks back to the previous part of the letter, and forward to Paul's warning.

In verses 4-5, Paul has said that every individual is responsible before God to respond obediently to the opportunities that God has given him or her. There is no way that such responsibility can be given away. But now Paul wants to make sure that this statement is not understood as promoting some kind of radical **individualism**. In order to avoid self-deception, we all need to submit ourselves to teachers who in turn have submitted themselves to other teachers.

All Christians need to have been those who have received "instruction in the word" (**v 6**). The Greek word for "anyone who receives instruction" is the *katechoumenos;* one who is **catechized**. This shows how important it was for new converts to be given a body of Christian doctrine (catechism), which was taught to them by an "instructor". Paul expects all new Christians to receive this basic discipleship teaching; and he wants them to "share all good things with [their] instructor (**v 6**). *Koinoneo* means "to share" or "to have fellowship". It could be read simply to mean that student and teacher must go about their task of instruction as full partners together. The student is not a passive pawn, and the teacher is not an imperious dictator.

But "all good things" almost certainly means financial support. It benefits both learner and teacher if the instructor is supported to do the job full-time. In this light, the word *koinoneo* becomes even richer, for the salary of a Christian teacher is not to be seen as a payment. Rather, it is a "fellowship". Just as teachers share the spiritual gifts God has given them with the learner, so the learners share the financial gifts God has given them with the teacher.

So we should give generously to our churches' staff teams. We should not be "consumers", who come to a church and simply plunder the benefits of it, without doing significant giving to that church. But this giving needs to be accompanied by the right attitude. Christian teaching is not just one more service to be paid for, but a rich fellowship and mutual sharing of the gifts of God.

> We should not be consumers, who come to a church to plunder the benefits of it.

Paul immediately follows this idea of supporting those who teach us the truth of the gospel with the warning: "Do not be deceived" (**v 7**). In some ways, this is the theme of the whole epistle of Galatians! Many of these young Christians had presumably been catechized by Paul himself; now they are in great danger of being deceived by the false teachers. Paul has argued that these teachers are not in "fellowship" with the Galatians; rather, they are using them to win honor and approval for themselves (4:17). By outlining the proper teacher-disciple relationship in **verse 6**, Paul is introducing his final appeal to resist these improper, false teachers. "Do not be deceived" is the beginning of Paul's last, climactic appeal to hold on to the truth.

Reap what you Sow

Next, Paul issues a stern warning. Some have called it "the law of great returns". Paul uses one of the most familiar experiences in the history of humankind—the agricultural processes of sowing and reaping. "Whatever a man sows, that he will also reap" (**v 7**, NKJV).

In farming or gardening, this is an **absolute** principle, and Paul appears to want us to see at least two aspects to it. First, *whatever* you sow, you will reap. If you sow tomato seeds, you will not get corn, no matter how much you want corn to grow! Second, whatever you sow, you *will* reap. Though the seed may lie in the ground to no apparent effect for a long time, it will come up. It is not the reaping that determines the harvest, but the sowing.

And this law of returns is as unstoppable in the moral and spiritual realm as it is in the agricultural one. "God cannot be mocked" (**v 7**)—He cannot be treated lightly. "The one who sows to please his sinful nature, from that nature will reap destruction" (**v 8**). This does not mean that God is a vengeful God, sitting in heaven looking to avenge any slights or insults. The image of sowing-reaping indicates that the process of moral consequences is much more natural and organic than that. Paul's reference to natural agriculture indicates that the moral universe has processes. Sin against God sets up strains in the fabric of the moral/spiritual universe, just as eating fatty foods sets up strains in the physical fabric of your heart. If you sow seed poorly, you reap a poor crop (and poverty). If you eat fatty foods, you reap a poor heart (and early death). If you give in to your sinful nature, you reap spiritual breakdown and destruction. The word "destruction" can also helpfully be rendered "corruption", or "disintegration". Paul is saying that sin makes things fall apart.

Sin makes things fall apart.

The destruction we reap comes from the breaking of the "fabric" of the moral universe, just as certain behavior can break the fabric and coherence of the physical. There are innumerable ways that sowing to please the sinful nature reaps destruction. The whole book of Proverbs is summed up by **Galatians 6 v 7-8**! To sow dishonesty breaks the fabric of relationships and creates the destruction of loneliness. To sow envy and jealousy breaks the fabric of contentment and creates the destruction of bitterness. And so on, for ever.

Whatever you sow, you will reap—sin always bears destruction, never joy and life. Whatever you sow, you *will* reap—sins will come home to roost; the consequences cannot be held off.

But Paul's warning here must be read in light of all the rest of his letter. He means something very specific when he speaks of "sow[ing] to please [the] sinful nature" (**v 8**). He has already showed that the sinful nature—*sarx*—is the part of our heart that wants to keep control of our lives by being our own savior and lord—which resists the gospel of free grace and seeks continually to earn our own righteousness.

Throughout the epistle, Paul has indicated that Christians can, and very often do, fall back into some kind of slavery to sin and, for that period of time or in that part of their lives, lose their grip on the gospel. They don't then cease to be Christians, saved by grace.

But Paul has also warned that if the gospel is rejected and works-righteousness formally and completely adopted, slavery and destruction will be complete. Both levels are probably in view here. If we as Christians fail to use the gospel, and live "in the flesh," trying to earn our salvation by other means, we will find a loss of coherence and joy and strength in our lives. And if anyone rejects the gospel and lives completely to the flesh, seeking and serving something other than Christ as their savior, then they will reap eternal destruction, rather than eternal life.

> The warning is stark; but the promise is wonderful.

The warning is stark; but the promise is wonderful. "The one who sows to please the Spirit, from the Spirit will reap eternal life" (**v 8**). If we live by the Spirit, we will enjoy the approval and assurance and fulfillment and joy of the Christian life now, and know that it will continue beyond death.

Sowing Well

So how can we be someone who "sows to please the Spirit" (**v 8**)? By obeying God out of the grateful joy that comes from knowing our status as children of God. When we do that, the idols which controlled our lives are disempowered and we are free to live for God.

Day by day, sowing to please the Spirit requires us to "not become weary in doing good" (**v 9**). There is always a delay between sowing and reaping. Especially, new farmers and gardeners will experience a lot of anxiety, watching over the **dormant** seed for weeks and weeks, and feeling it will never come up. But it always comes up in the end. Paul has warned sinners that, though it may seem for a long time that your sin hasn't found you out, eventually it will. Now he wants to encourage those who are living for Christ. People who do good will see the fruits and benefits—eventually.

Paul is encouraging these young Christians not to lose heart because, just as inexperienced gardeners might fail to water and weed in their discouragement over the slow-growing seed, so Christians might fail to **persevere** in their service and ministry. A lack of follow-through in ministry can stunt the "harvest", just as it does in gardening.

What is this "doing good" sowing? It is to "do good to all people, especially to those who belong to the family of believers" (**v 10**). This is sweeping and comprehensive in its simplicity. First, it shows what the Christian life is all about; not primarily meetings, programs or even conversions, but doing good to the person in front of you, giving him or her what is best for them.

Second, the word "doing" shows that we are to give them whatever love discerns as their needs. Of course, we share the gospel and **evangelize**, but only as a means to the end of loving them. (We don't love them as a means to the end of converting them!) But the word "doing" means that we must not confine ourselves to **evangelism** and discipling. We are to love in deed as well as in word. We are to give them any aid that is necessary to meet any need within our power to meet, whether it is material, social or spiritual. This little phrase shows that Christian ministry includes helping at a rehabilitation home just as much as explaining to someone how to give your life to Christ.

> "Doing" means that we must not confine ourselves to evangelism and discipling.

This love is to be directed to "all people" (**v 10**). So we don't get immediately overwhelmed, Paul has already added "as we have opportunity"—we're not expected personally to meet all the needs of all people! We should look around us and see who we are near and where we are.

But supremely, this love is to be given to "the family of believers" (**v 10**), a wonderful phrase that shows all Christians are a family. Christians are all brothers and sisters in God's household (4:5). We must do good intensely with those who are in fellowship with us.

This is the lifestyle from which, "if we do not give up", we "will reap a harvest"—real, fulfilling, lasting life (**v 9**). In the short run, such a life demands a tremendous number of sacrifices. You bind your heart up emotionally to people who are unstable, so you experience great distress that you could have avoided. You cut yourself off from many options that you could have if you weren't in ministry relationships. You have less money since you are giving very generously to individuals and ministries and causes. The costs are many, but the rewards, Paul hints, are as much greater as the value of the harvest is greater than the cost of the seed! First, we often get the direct and deep satisfaction of seeing changed lives (see Matthew 9:37). Second, we may get the direct and deep satisfaction of seeing families and communities, even cities, becoming good and happy places to live. Third, we may even see people whose burdens we've been bearing become burden bearers; changed lives which begin to change other lives.

But we need to realize that there are deeper harvests that happen even when we don't meet with much outward success. We will find our own character changing deeply through ministry. Our consciences will be clear and our hearts happier, since we're less self-indulgent. We'll develop a less selfish and more satisfied character, which will serve us well when we are under pressure. We may not reap quickly, and we may not see all that we reap; but we can know that there is a great harvest for those who sow to please the Spirit.

Questions for reflection

1. Can you think of times in your own life when sowing to please your sinful nature has forced you to reap "destruction"?

2. How are you reaping to please the Spirit in your specific set of God-given circumstances?

3. How have these verses motivated you to "do good to all people"? Are there any particular changes the Spirit is moving you to make?

PART TWO

In his own Hand

Now Paul seizes the pen from his scribe. We've seen throughout the letter that this is no theological treatise—it is a letter from a man who deeply loves the men and women he is writing to. Here is his last appeal, his last invitation to keep trusting the gospel for salvation and living it out day by day, and he decides to "write to you with my own hand!" (**v 11**).

First, he wants to convince them that real Christianity is a matter of inward change, not external observance. It is substantial, not superficial. Again, he focuses on the motives of the false teachers. They "want to make a good impression outwardly" (**v 12**).

Paul has already said that the preaching of the gospel is terribly offensive to the human heart (5:11-12). People find it insulting to be told that they are too weak and sinful to do anything to contribute to their salvation. The gospel is offensive to liberal-minded people, who charge the gospel with intolerance, because it states that the only way to be saved is through the cross. The gospel is offensive to conservative-minded people, because it states that, without the cross, "good" people are in as much trouble as "bad" people. Ultimately, the gospel is offensive because the cross stands against all schemes of self-salvation. The world appreciates "religion" and "morality" in general. The world thinks that moral religion is a good thing for society. But the world is offended by the cross. So people who love the cross are "persecuted" (**v 12**).

The cross is by nature offensive! And we can only grasp its sweetness if we first grapple with its offense. If someone understands the cross, it is either the greatest thing in their life, or it is

> We can only grasp the gospel's sweetness if we first grapple with its offense.

repugnant to them. If it is neither of those two things, they haven't understood it.

The false savior the Judaizers are worshiping is approval. That's what is going on under their legalistic teaching. "The only reason they [teach what they do] is to avoid being persecuted for the cross of Christ" (**v 12**). They want to "boast" (**v 13**). They have gotten into religion for the fame, prestige and honor it can bring them in the world. Their ministry, as we saw in 4:17-18, is a form of self-salvation.

As a result of this concern for appearances and acceptance by the world, the false teachers are offering a religion that mainly focuses on externals and behavior (circumcision and the ceremonial law), rather than internal change of heart, motives and character. The gospel is inside-out: an inner change of heart leads to a new motivation for and conduct of behavior. They are outside-out: focusing on behavior, never dealing with the heart, and always remaining superficial.

Paul again makes the most telling critique of this way of religion: "Not even those who are circumcised obey the law" (**v 13**). On its own terms, biblical legalism cannot work. If we really read the law and see what it commands (eg: "Love your neighbor as yourself", 5:13-14), we will see that we cannot possibly save ourselves by obeying it. A religion based on externals and behavior as a way of salvation may prompt pride and bring popularity, but it cannot deliver the eternal life it promises.

What are You Boasting About?

Ultimately, Paul says, the heart of your religion is what you boast in. What, at bottom, is the reason that you think you are in a right relationship with God?

If the cross is just a help, but you have to complete your salvation with good works, it is really *your works* which make the difference between your being headed for heaven or not headed for heaven. Therefore, you "boast about your flesh" (**v 13**), your own efforts.

What an attractive-sounding message: to be able to pat yourself on the back for having reserved a place for yourself in heaven!

But if you understand the gospel, you "boast" exclusively and only in the cross. Our identity, our self-image, is based on what gives us a sense of dignity and significance—what we boast in. Religion leads us to boast in something about us. The gospel leads us to boast in the cross of Jesus. That means our identity in Jesus is confident and secure—we do "boast"!—yet humbly, based on a profound sense of our flaws and neediness.

So the gospel can be well summarized in one remarkable sentence: "May I never boast except in the cross of our Lord Jesus Christ, through which the world has been crucified to me, and I to the world" (**v 14**).

I am saved solely and wholly because of Christ's work, not mine. He has reserved a place in heaven for me, given freely to me by Him. I "never boast"—I take no credit for my standing with God—"except in the cross"; what Christ has done is now something I "boast" in. To boast is to joyously **exult**, and to have high confidence, in something. To know you are saved by Christ's work alone brings a joyous "boasting" confidence; not a self-confidence, but Christ-confidence.

And if I truly boast in Christ alone, there is a stunning turnaround in my life. The world is dead to me. First, as Stott says, the Christian does not need to care what the world thinks of them. But Guthrie probably gets closer to Paul's gist when he says:

> "The natural world ... has ceased to have any claims on us".
>
> (*Galatians*, page 151)

> If I truly boast in Christ alone, there is a stunning turnaround in my life.

Paul is telling the Christian that there is nothing in the world now that has any power over them. Notice he does not say that the world is dead, but that it is dead *to him*. The gospel destroys its power. Why? As we have been saying all along, if nothing in the world is where I locate my righteousness or salvation, if there is nothing in the world that I boast in, then there is nothing in the world that controls me—nothing that I *must* have.

Paul is not saying that I must have nothing to do with the people and things of the world. Ironically, if I must have nothing to do with the world and must separate from it, then the world still has quite a lot of power over me! Paul means that the Christian is now free to enjoy the world, because he no longer needs to fear it, nor to worship it.

> The Christian is free to enjoy the world, because he no longer needs to fear or worship it.

So Paul restates what he said back in 5:6: "Neither circumcision nor uncircumcision means anything; but a new creation" (**6:15**). Religious or moral attainments, and religious or moral failures, are irrelevant when it comes to salvation, because it is not about what I have done, but about what Christ has done.

Because of the gospel of Christ crucified, Paul says, I do not feel inferior to or intimidated by anyone—circumcision means nothing. And because of the gospel, I do not feel superior to or scornful of anyone—uncircumcision means nothing.

All that matters is that, through Christ crucified, we are made a "new creation" (**v 15**). The gospel changes my future, giving me a place in Christ's perfected re-creation. And the gospel changes my present, giving me a whole new self-image and whole new way of relating to everyone.

"A new creation" in **verse 15** is the parallel to "faith working by love" in 5:6. Paul's point is that the two are essentially the same thing. The gospel creates a new motivation for obedience—grateful love arising from a faith view of what Christ has done. This new motivation renews us from the inside out. It is a new birth, a supernatural transformation of character, a new creation.

So **verses 14-15** sum up what it means to rely on what Christ has done, rather than on what I am doing. Paul says: *The gospel changes what I fundamentally boast in—it changes the whole basis for my identity. Nothing in the whole world has any power over me—I am free at last to enjoy the world, for I do not need the world. I feel neither inferior to anyone nor superior to anyone, and I am being made all over into someone and something entirely new.*

A Life of Peace

If verses 14-15 sum up chapter 5, **verse 16** (which, following such an emotional and stunning sentence, is easy to miss!) encapsulates what Paul was saying in chapter 3. Here, he calls living by the gospel a "rule" (**v 16**)—it is a way of life, a foundation of everything. Anyone who sets the gospel of Christ as their "rule", he says, will find "peace and mercy". And they will be members of "the Israel of God". Christians are all Abraham's children, heirs to God's promises to him.

Paul concludes by pointing to the fact that "I bear on my body the marks of Jesus" (**v 17**). What are these? Probably he is referring to the literal scars he had from the torture, imprisonments and beatings he had received for the sake of Christ. The teachers of the false, popular, self-salvation gospel had none of these, because the world loved to hear their message. But Paul is a true minister, a true apostle, as he argued in chapters 1 and 2. *Do not doubt me,* he says: *I have the real marks of apostolic authority—not greatness and riches, but signs of suffering and weakness.*

"Grace" is the entry point to, the way to continue with, and all we will ever need in, the Christian life.

And then he signs off. But even here, Paul is reminding the Galatians of the message of his letter. "The grace of our Lord Jesus Christ" (**v 18**) is the entry point to, and the way to continue with, and all we will ever need in, the Christian life. We begin by grace, by being justified by faith in what Christ has done. We continue by grace, not by anything we do. This gospel of grace is what the Galatians need to know, and love, in "your spirit". It is not a set of abstract truths. It is a way of life, of deeply fulfilling, secure life now, and of eternal life to come. Amen.

Questions for reflection

1. How does verse 14 thrill you? How does it challenge you?

2. In which areas of your life are you knowing the peace of living by the gospel? In which are you forfeiting this peace by living for the world's approval?

3. If you had to sum up the message of the whole book of Galatians in a few words, what would you say?

GLOSSARY

Abraham: the ancestor of the nation of Israel, and the man God made a binding agreement (covenant) with. God promised to make his family into a great nation, give them a land, and bring blessing to all nations through one of his descendants (see Genesis 12:1-3).

Absolute: total, permanent, definite.

Affections: the inclinations of our hearts. Our affections are what drive and shape our emotions.

Alienated: to become enemies of and hostile to someone eg: Christ.

Allegory: a story which is a picture of a deeper meaning or truth. For example, John Bunyan's *Pilgrim's Progress* is an allegory of becoming and living as a Christian.

Amen: true.

Amoral: to be unconcerned about whether something is right or wrong. This is different from immoral, which is to not conform to a generally accepted standard of right and wrong.

Analogy: a comparison between two things, usually using one of them to explain or clarify the other.

Antioch: a city 300 miles north of Jerusalem in what is now southern Turkey, and the site of the first church where a majority of the members were Gentiles. Antioch was the place where Jesus' followers were first called "Christians" (see Acts 11:19-26).

Aorist tense: referring to something that happened in the past and at a particular point in time, eg: "David hit Tyrone".

Arabia: a barren desert area east of Israel. In Galatians 4:25, Paul is not saying Mount Sinai is literally in Arabia (it isn't!)—he is using Arabia as a metaphor for barrenness.

Barren: unable to have children.

Catechized: taught the central principles of the Christian faith by asking and answering questions.

Circumcision: God told the men among His people in the Old Testament to be circumcised as a way to show physically that they knew and trusted Him, and belonged to the people of God (see Genesis 17).

Commission: duty, responsibility, appointment.

Concubines: women who live with a man but who have a lower status than his wife (or wives); a sort of official live-in lover.

Conform: change to be like someone or something.

Convoluted: complicated.

Damascus road: the road between Jerusalem (in modern-day Israel) and Damascus (in modern-day Syria), a distance of 135 miles. It was on this road that the risen Jesus appeared to the Apostle Paul (also called Saul). Paul became a Christian as a result of this experience (see Acts 9:1-19).

Denominational: a branch of the church. Eg: Presbyterian, Southern Baptist, Anglican/Episcopalian, Methodist.

Doctrine: the study of what is true about God.

Dormant: temporarily inactive.

Egalitarian: the belief that all people are fundamentally of equal value.

Emboldens: gives courage to.

Epistle: a New Testament letter eg: Galatians, Romans, 1 Corinthians.

Evangelize, evangelism: to tell people the gospel of Jesus Christ.

Exult: show and feel happiness and excitement.

Functional: actual, real.

Gentiles: people who are not ethnically Jewish.

Gifts: God-given talents or abilities (see 1 Corinthians 12:4-11).

Glorification: the moment when one of God's people is made perfect, like Christ, and welcomed into God's eternal kingdom.

Gospel: an announcement, often translated "good news". When the Roman Emperor sent a proclamation around the empire declaring a victory or achievement, this was called a "gospel". The gospel is good news to be believed, not good advice to be followed.

Grace: unmerited favor. In the Bible, "grace" is usually used to describe how God treats His people. Because God is full of grace, He gives believers eternal life (Ephesians 2:4-8); He also gives them gifts to use to serve His people (Ephesians 4:7, 11-13).

Heretical: a belief which directly opposes the biblical gospel (ie: the opposite of orthodox). A heretic is someone who, despite being challenged, continues to hold to heretical beliefs.

Holy: totally pure; set apart.

Impart: give.

Incarnation: the coming of the divine Son of God as a human, in the person of Jesus Christ.

Individualism: the view that we are individuals who are not part of, don't need to rely on, and are not accountable to any larger body of people.

Jerusalem: the capital of Israel, and the site of the temple. In Old Testament times, this was the center of life and worship for God's people. Often, Bible writers use "Jerusalem" to stand for "Israel" or "the people of God".

John the Baptist: Jesus' cousin, and a prophet whose role was to announce that God's chosen King (Christ) would shortly be arriving in

Israel, and to call people to turn back to God as their Ruler in preparation for Christ's arrival. See Mark 1:4-8.

Kosher: food that satisfied the requirements of the Old Testament food laws.

Legalism: a way of living that obeys certain rules in the belief that keeping these requirements will earn some form of blessing (for example, eternal life or worldly wealth).

License: living however you want to.

Licentious: living according to feeling, rather than principles, particularly with regard to sex.

Mediator: someone who brings two enemies together and makes it possible for them to be friends again.

Metaphor: an image which is used to explain something, but which is not to be taken literally (eg: "The news was a dagger to his heart").

Mosaic law: the Old Testament laws, which God gave Moses in the books of Exodus, Leviticus, Numbers and Deuteronomy, and which lay out how Israel are to relate to God and live as His people.

Moses: the leader of God's people at the time when God brought them out of slavery in Egypt. God communicated His law (including the Ten Commandments) through Moses, and under his leadership guided them toward the land He had promised to give them.

Mount Sinai: a mountain in the desert between Egypt and the promised land (which came to be called Israel). Here, God revealed Himself to Moses, established His covenant with Israel, and gave His people His law (see Exodus 19). Mount Sinai is also called Mount Horeb.

Objective: a truth which is based on facts, not feelings, eg: "I am married to this woman".

Orthodox: standard, accepted Christian teaching.

Pagan(ism): someone who doesn't know and worship the true God.

Parable: a memorable story told by Jesus to illustrate a truth about Him and/or His kingdom.

Parallelism: close similarity, connection.

Passive process: something that happens without you doing anything (the opposite of "active"). For example, ageing is a passive process!

Persevere: continue to think or do something despite facing difficulty.

Pharisees: a Jewish group who lived by strict observance of both God's Old Testament law and Jewish tradition. The Pharisees thought their law-observance made them right with God (mistakenly—see, for example, Jesus' parable in Luke 18 v 9-14). Paul himself had been a Pharisee before he became a Christian (Acts 23:6; 26:4-5).

Permissiveness: living however you want to.

Polygamy: having more than one wife at the same time.

Predestination: the doctrine that God has chosen to save certain people out of His great and undeserved love, rather than on the basis of their character or actions (see, for instance, Ephesians 1:4-6).

Prodigal: wasteful, spends money recklessly or lavishly.

Prophets: people used by God to communicate a message to people.

Reborn: someone who has put their faith in Christ and been given new, eternal life (see John 3:5-8; 1 Peter 1:3-5).

Relativize/Relativistic: to have an outlook based on the belief that truth and morality are not a matter of absolutes, which hold for every person in every context in every age, but are products of someone's culture and/or experience, and therefore change. So something can be wrong for you, but right for me.

Righteous/Righteousness: in Galatians, it means the status of being in right relationship with God.

Sanctified: made pure; changed to become like Christ (see Romans 8:29).

Secular: to live without reference to God or any religion, and to reject any notion of spirituality.

Sinai covenant of law: the binding agreement made by God, with His people, as they traveled from Egypt to the promised land.

Sins: thoughts, words and actions that come from rejecting God, and worshiping something else in His place.

Sovereign: royal, all-powerful.

Speaking in tongues: a spiritual gift of speaking in other, sometimes non-earthly, languages eg: Acts 2; 1 Corinthians 12:7-11.

Subjective: something which is based on feelings and opinions. Eg: "She is the most beautiful woman in the world" is a subjective opinion.

Substitutionary: an act that involves a replacement, where someone (or something) stands in or is substituted for another.

Supernaturally: describing something which cannot happen in the natural way the world works.

Tenet: a principle or belief.

Testimony: the true story of how God brought an individual to faith in Jesus.

The Twelve: the twelve apostles. These were Jesus' twelve disciples, minus Judas, who betrayed Him, plus Matthias, who was chosen to take the place of Judas (see Mark 3:13-19; Acts 1:15-26).

Theology: the study of what is true about God.

Traits: qualities or distinguishing features.

Transgressions: sins. Literally, the word means "stepped across a line".

Vacuum: a space with nothing in it, and which nature will always try to fill.

Works-righteousness: the view that a person's works (ie: thoughts, words and actions) can bring them into right relationship with God.

Yoke: a piece of wood fastened over the necks of animals and attached to a plow or cart that they are to pull.

Zealous: to be extremely passionate, enthusiastic and uncompromising about something.

APPENDIX: The Recent Debate

Recently a "new perspective" has developed over what the term "works of the law" means in 2:16; 3:2, 5, 10.

Many interpreters believe Paul is talking about the Mosaic ceremonial law *only*—circumcision, the dietary laws, the other laws which are about keeping ritually "clean". In this view, "works of the law" is not moral performance in general, but the adoption of Jewish cultural customs and ethnic boundary markers. And so the Judaizers are not urging the Galatian Christians to adopt a works-righteousness system of salvation (ie: the idea that you must obey particular laws in order to be right with God). Instead, the argument goes, these teachers are insisting that Gentile Christians take on Jewish ethnic markers and become culturally Jewish.

So in this "new perspective" the Judaizers are not legalists, but nationalists. And Paul is therefore not opposing salvation-by-works, but rather racial and ethnic exclusivity. This means that Paul's purpose in the book of Galatians is to insist that all races and classes sit down equally at the "table of God", because we are all one in Christ.

I have taken extensive time to weigh the pros and cons of this "new perspective", and I believe it is very helpful in several ways, but that it cannot overthrow the essence of the historic, classic approach. This is not the place for an in-depth analysis, and what follows is certainly not intended to be any sort of last word, but here are my brief conclusions…

You cannot ultimately drive a wedge between nationalism and legalism as if they are two separate things. Indeed, the book of Galatians addresses a controversy that had at its heart a racial/ethnic pride and superiority. In 2:11-15, Peter is clearly in the grip of this, having been influenced by the Judaizers (2:12). These teachers were pressing Jewish cultural boundary markers on Gentile Christian converts. And so, works of the law probably does include this.

But nationalism is a form of legalism. Legalism is adding *anything* to Jesus Christ as a requirement for full acceptance with God. A moral superiority that comes from good works *or* from racial and cultural pedigree grows out of the same spiritual root. The gospel is that we are saved through what Christ does, and not by what we do or are. So when the Judaizers called the Gentile converts to the works of the law, they were calling them to adopt Jewish cultural identity, but they were *also* pulling them into a form of self-salvation. Human achievement was becoming the basis for their standing with God.

This is seen in how Paul speaks of the "works of the law" in Romans (where the term is used in Romans 3:20, 27, 28.) On the one hand, this term does bear ethnic significance for Jews. It was by works that Israel sought to establish itself in its relationship with God (Romans 9:30 – 10:3). But on the other hand, Paul associates the works of the law with "boasting" (Romans 3:27-28).

This is key, because throughout the Scriptures "boasting" is used about what you rely on and have pride in (see Jeremiah 9:23-24; 1 Corinthians 1:31). Paul says that boasting in, or trusting in, yourself is what underlies the works of the law. So while works of the law can mean relying on (or boasting in) nationalism, it cannot *only* mean that; nationalism is a form of self-salvation, or legalism. And it is *this* that Paul means by the phrase "works of the law".

So, ultimately, we must still read the book of Galatians as Paul's defense of the gospel of free grace against winning God's favor by human accomplishment or status. The new perspective can't dislodge the classic understanding of Galatians. But this debate over the term "works of the law" is nonetheless helpful to us in two ways.

First, it shows us how subtly the gospel can be undermined from within the Christian church and community. The new perspective shows us that the Judaizers were not full-bore legalists who flatly rejected Christ. As we'll see, they were not saying: *You don't need Jesus. If you are a good person, you will go to heaven anyway.* It is highly unlikely the Galatians would have been duped by such a blatant contradiction of the gospel message that saved them.

Instead, the Judaizers were saying: *Jesus was critical and crucial to getting you saved, of course, but faith in Him alone is not enough to grow you into full acceptance with God. You will now have to adopt the full range of Mosaic ceremonial and cultural customs.* This is much more subtle. It is saying: *You were related to God by grace, but now you have to grow in Him by trying very, very hard to obey all these particular rules* (3:1-5).

In the same way, spirit-deadening moralism would not grow in our churches by blatant, obvious denials of the doctrine of justification by faith alone. This truth is much more likely to be undermined in new forms of demanding cultural conformity or other approaches, which in our own culture and time are just as subtle as the Judaizers were in theirs.

Second, this debate shows us that the book of Galatians has been read too much as a rather academic debate about doctrine. But Paul is not only concerned about a breakdown in the doctrinal beliefs of individuals. He also has a deep concern about a breakdown in Christian unity and community. It is important to see how much the book of Galatians is addressed to the problems of racial and cultural exclusivity, and other social aspects of Christian living. The truths of the gospel are not matters only for the ivory tower, for lecture rooms and doctoral theses; they are fundamental to everyday life, in the heart and the home, with congregation members and co-workers.

BIBLIOGRAPHY

■ Sinclair B. Ferguson, *Children of the Living God* (Banner of Truth, 1989)

■ Donald Guthrie, *Galatians* in the New Century Commentary series (Marshall, Morgan & Scott, 1973)

■ C.S. Lewis, *Surprised by Joy: The Shape of My Early Life* (Houghton Mifflin Harcourt, revised ed 1995)

■ Richard Lovelace, *Dynamics of Spiritual Life* (IVP, 1979)

■ Martin Luther, *Commentary on the Epistle to the Galatians* (Suzeteo Enterprises, 2011)

■ Douglas J. Moo, *The Epistle to the Romans* in The New International Commentary series (Eerdmans, 1996)

■ J.I. Packer, *God's Words* (IVP, 1981)

■ David Powlison, "Idols of the Heart and 'Vanity Fair'" in *The Journal of Biblical Counseling* (Volume 13, Number 2, Winter 1995)

■ John Stott, *The Message of Acts* in The Bible Speaks Today series (IVP, 1968)

■ John Stott, *The Message of Galatians* in The Bible Speaks Today series (IVP, 1968)

Galatians for...
Bible-study Groups

Timothy Keller's **Good Book Guide** to Galatians is the companion to this resource, helping groups of Christians to explore, discuss and apply Paul's letter together. Seven studies, each including investigation, apply, getting personal, pray and explore more sections, take you through the whole of Galatians. Each Good Book Guide includes a concise Leader's Guide at the back.

Find out more at:
www.thegoodbook.com/good-book-guides

Daily Devotionals

Explore daily devotional helps you open up the Scriptures and will encourage and equip you in your walk with God. Available as a quarterly booklet, *Explore* is also available as an app, where you can download Dr Keller's notes on Galatians, alongside contributions from trusted Bible teachers including Mark Dever, Tim Chester, Mike McKinley, Stephen Witmer and Ray Ortlund.

Find out more at:
www.thegoodbook.com/explore

More For You
Coming Soon...

Galatians For You is the first title in the new *God's Word For You series*. Forthcoming titles by Timothy Keller include:

- **Judges For You**
- **Psalms For You**
- **Romans 1 - 7 For You**
- **Romans 8 - 16 For You**
- **2 Timothy For You**
- **1 John For You**

Find out more about these resources, and more *God's Word For You* titles by other pastors, at:
www.thegoodbook.com/for-you

Romans 1 - 7 For You

"The gospel's power is seen in its ability to completely change minds, hearts, lives, perceptions, relationships… everything. But most of all, its power is in its ability to do what no other power on earth can do—save us, reconcile us to God, and guarantee us a place in the kingdom of God forever. Truly, 'it is the power of God for salvation' (Romans 1:16)."

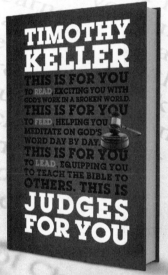

Judges For You

"Our era can be characterized by the phrase: 'Everyone did as he saw fit' (Judges 21:25). So the book of Judges has much to say to the individualism and paganism of our own day. And it has much to say about the God of grace, who works in the worst of situations, and who triumphs over the stupidest of actions."

Good Book Guides
for small group studies

Ezekiel: The God of Glory

Tim Chester
Pastor of The Crowded House, Sheffield, UK

"Then they will know that I am the Lord" is the repeated message of Ezekiel. In a world of false hopes that will ultimately fail, this is a message for everyone.

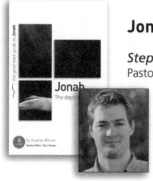

Jonah: The Depths of Grace

Stephen Witmer
Pastor of Pepperell Christian Fellowship, MA

The book of Jonah reveals to us the depths of God's grace, both to "outsiders" and to "insiders". It shows us God's compassion for the lost and His patience with His wayward people.

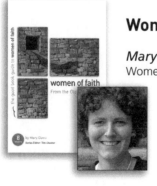

Women of Faith

Mary Davis
Women's Ministry Director, St Nicholas Church, Tooting, UK

Examine the lives and experiences of seven women from ancient Israel; their flaws, faith, struggles and solutions.

"We're excited to use Good Book Guides at our church. They are clear and easy-to-use, and teach people to dig deeper into Scripture for themselves."

Joshua Harris, Senior Pastor, Covenant Life Church, Gaithersburg, Maryland

1 Corinthians: Challenging Church

Mark Dever
Senior Pastor of Capitol Hill Baptist Church in Washington DC; President of 9Marks Ministries

The church in Corinth was full of life, and full of problems. As Paul challenges these Christians, you'll see how you can help shape your own church to become truly gospel-centered.

Ephesians: God's Big Plan for Christ's New People

Thabiti Anyabwile
Senior Pastor, First Baptist Church, Grand Cayman

If we would be healthy Christians, we would be wise to build our lives around the kind of church that emerges from this book.

See the full range of 35 titles at:
www.thegoodbook.com/goodbookguides

thegoodbook
COMPANY
Opening up the Bible

At The Good Book Company, we are dedicated to helping Christians and local churches grow. We believe that God's growth process always starts with hearing clearly what He has said to us through His timeless word—the Bible.

Ever since we opened our doors in 1991, we have been striving to produce resources that honor God in the way the Bible is used. We have grown to become an international provider of user-friendly resources to the Christian community, with believers of all backgrounds and denominations using our Bible studies, books, evangelistic resources, DVD-based courses and training events.

We want to equip ordinary Christians to live for Christ day by day, and churches to grow in their knowledge of God, their love for one another, and the effectiveness of their outreach.

Call us for a discussion of your needs or visit one of our local websites for more information on the resources and services we provide.

North America: www.thegoodbook.com
UK & Europe: www.thegoodbook.co.uk
Australia: www.thegoodbook.com.au
New Zealand: www.thegoodbook.co.nz

North America: 866 244 2165
UK & Europe: 0333 123 0880
Australia: (02) 6100 4211
New Zealand (+64) 3 343 1990

www.christianityexplored.org
Our partner site is a great place for those exploring the Christian faith, with a clear explanation of the good news, powerful testimonies and answers to difficult questions.

One life. What's it all about?